15p

AFTER YOU, COLUMBUS

AFTER YOU, COLUMBUS

BY

HAKON MIELCHE

LONDON   EDINBURGH   GLASGOW
WILLIAM HODGE AND COMPANY, LIMITED

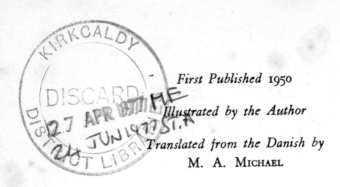

First Published 1950

Illustrated by the Author

Translated from the Danish by
M. A. MICHAEL

TRANSLATOR'S NOTE

Rather than submit the extracts from Columbus' "Journal" to double translation, I have used the scholarly and most excellent version prepared by Mr. Van Wyck Brooks and published in 1925 under the title "Christopher Columbus— The Journal of his First Voyage to America" by Messrs. Jarrolds, to whom I wish to express my gratitude.

Made and Printed in Great Britain by William Hodge & Co., Ltd., London, Edinburgh and Glasgow

CONTENTS

CONTENTS—*Continued*

LIST OF ILLUSTRATIONS

LIST OF ILLUSTRATIONS—*Continued*

CHAPTER I

I Buy the Boat

SHE was bought in Bergen, and it was I who bought
her. To be accurate, I bought her, but it was Allers
Magazine in Oslo that paid out the money, for things
were such in that year of grace 1948, thirty years after
the war to end all wars, and three years after that to
ensure us the inestimable gifts of peace, that a Dane
could not buy a new hat in Norway, nor a Norwegian
buy a toothbrush in Denmark, until he had obtained
the permission of both countries' national banks to
acquire, export and import the necessary foreign
currency. With such difficulties in the way of acquiring
small personal articles, you can imagine the obstacles
to be overcome when it was a boat you wanted to buy.

She was a boat of 24 tons and therefore did not
require to be registered in either the Danish or Norwegian shipping register. Being a pleasure craft and
to the professional and inexpert eye obviously unsuited to the carriage of coal, fruit or cattle other than
in home waters, I would like to have registered her in
the yacht register, since a yacht certificate entitles you
to a number of privileges all over the world ; but I
could not register her with the Norwegian Yacht Club,
because I was not a Norwegian, and though the Danish
Club was only too willing to have me as a member, it
could not enrol the boat since she was Norwegian.

A   I

The boat's home port was Oslo. That was entered in all our papers. So, I bought a Norwegian flag, engaged a Danish crew, if only to avoid difficulties in paying their wages which would otherwise have had to be calculated in various currencies, and sailed for Denmark with my booty.

When we arrived in Denmark, Norwegians came streaming up from all the ships near us and welcomed us in their mother tongue. We answered them shame-facedly in Danish, feeling rather like boys caught red-handed in the neighbour's apple tree. Then the Norwegians looked from us to our flag and back again, and demanded an explanation.

It was an uncomfortable enough position to be in, but I realized that it was only the beginning. In imagination I could already see us putting into some distant tropic port with the Norwegian colours fluttering bravely in the Trades, and Norwegians who had not been home for a generation or more saddling their horses fifty miles inland when the news reached them and fighting their way through scrub and jungle to come and greet us, only to find that we didn't have a single thing from Norway to offer them, none of their dried cod or whey-cheese, not even a bottle of Loyten's gin. Our boat might well degenerate into a new Greenland saga. Had the Norwegian National Bank envisaged such a consequence?

I telegraphed to the bank. I wrote to it. Could not the Danish Allers Magazine be given permission to transfer the purchase price to its sister company in Oslo? The Danish National Bank was ready to agree. The Danish shipping and all other authorities were ready to pass our papers through at lightning speed and have the boat made Danish. But the Bank of Norway was adamant : there could be no question of a transfer. If we wanted to buy a boat in Norway, we could do so, and we could take her away and hoist whatever flag we liked—as long as we paid in dollars. They might just as well have asked for a slice of the moon, or for the half of Molotov's moustache ; for I personally had not received as much as five cents of the Marshall Loan.

So we gave up and sailed without a flag. As soon as we were outside Danish waters, I hoisted the Danish flag, the Danish yacht flag with its split and stars. That was piracy and I knew the punishment : I would be hauled up to the yard-arm and left to dangle when I got home again, but at least I should have spared Norwegians in the distant tropics a great disappointment.

I felt a little anxious the first time we put into a foreign port and the officials sat beneath the flapping split-flag examining our papers and saw that our home port was Oslo. However, I soon got over that, for no one ever protested and many of them wrote down in their papers " Oslo, Denmark " and under-lined it three times. In Guernsey two customs men had a bet whether the flag was Swedish or Finnish, and it was only in Lisbon, where everybody is sus-picious, that one harbour official looked up his books and discovered that our flag was Danish, but Oslo in Norway. However, I kept my head, produced my membership card from the Royal Danish Yacht Club and told him that of course the boat was Norwegian,

but I had chartered her and didn't he know that yachts had to hoist the flag of the club to which the master belonged? After that he shuffled off—richer by 20 escudos than when he came.

All the same, we did occasionally feel that we ought to hoist the Jolly Roger—but that's enough about the boat's nationality.

The actual purchase was made in the Grand Hotel Terminus in Bergen, where I handed over the cheque standing by a fireplace on which stood a lovely model of Christopher Columbus' *Santa Maria*. The boat's name was *Edirene* and she had quite an exciting little history, part of which I later managed to piece together. She was built in Portsmouth in 1904, so we were of the same age, my boat and I. She was built as a yacht and used as such by people called Archer. However, the family was not connected with the world-famous Anglo-Norwegian shipbuilder so I could not boast of having a Colin Archer boat, much as I should have liked to. The Archer family used her for long trips up and down the coast of Britain, and, as they had a holiday home in the Norwegian skerries, *Edirene* also crossed the North Sea and Skaggerak and ploughed the Atlantic. The ship broker from whom I bought her had in his possession a log book from a voyage to India kept by a Lieutenant Archer, R.N., and this gave rise to the legend that *Edirene* had been in India. Enquiries made in England showed that it was highly improbable she ever had been, though a younger member of the Archer family had been in the Royal Navy and done a turn of duty in Indian waters. The log book may just have been his diary.

At the outbreak of the first world war the Archer family sold *Edirene* to a Norwegian brewer who sailed her till Norway introduced prohibition. When that happened, there wasn't much trade in his beer, so he sold her to a Norwegian captain who tried his hand at smuggling and ran spirits in her. Things went well at first, but his luck did not hold and in the end the Norwegian Customs caught him, confiscated his boat and put her up for auction after destroying all her papers. At that time the Norwegian Aluminium Company was in need of a vessel to take passengers and goods from Bergen to its factory up the fjord.  So the Company bought *Edirene*, removed her booms, gaffs and sails, installed two powerful American Wolverine engines amidships, bored two heavy propeller shafts through the whole hull, erected a smoking lounge aft, and a wheel-room like a summer-house on an allotment for'ard in front of the lounge, installed an engine-room telegraph, and put a great searchlight in the bows, and set her plying between Hoyanger and Bergen as a twin-screwed motorboat. The open seas had lost one more storm bird, and Bergen received an additional tram.

When I met *Edirene* she was lying among dirty packet-boats alongside the quay in Bergen harbour, herself as dirty as her neighbours. She stank of oil and she dripped oil. Her teak gunwale had been brutally painted a deadly dull dark brown colour. Her rigging had rusted beneath a layer of aluminium paint, while ropes and sails lay forgotten in a damp loft somewhere up the fjord and had not been touched for the last sixteen years. That was the state she was in.

She was a sorry sight indeed, but there was no denying her breeding. I am not a sailor, and I never shall be; but I have drawn a lot in my life and that has given me an eye for line. This and several years spent in ships has given me a certain faculty for judging a ship's or a boat's build, enough at any rate for me to recognize the moment I saw her that I was standing face to face with a thoroughbred of the seas.

I looked and looked, and the more I looked the more I felt that perhaps were she to be restored to her original form, were one carefully and tenderly to remove the scars and ravages of the years, perhaps it would be possible one day to sail her out from this narrow fjord, where she had laboured like a cart-horse, and let the salt spray of the ocean spurt up over her deck and once again allow her to unfurl her white wings and set course for a horizon that was not bounded by steep mountains. Could I bring that about, I should feel that I had set a caged bird free. And perhaps my reward would be that I could link my fate to hers for a time and follow her into adventure and to distant lands beyond some far horizon.

When I was much younger we sailed around the world, or at least we made an honourable attempt to do so, in a boat of about the same size as *Edirene*, the good old *Monsoon* whose timbers have been rotting on a coral reef in the Solomon Islands these fifteen years and more. *Monsoon* was heavier and broader, of old French fishing-cutter stock. *Edirene* was of nobler lineage; but they were both sea-birds meant to roam the ocean. I went back to my hotel and rang up my paper, told them that here in Bergen was an opportunity to go back to those early days when we had said to each other " Let's see if the world is round ". They were understanding people, and so that is how the boat came to be bought in Bergen.

The day after I had bought her, the shipwrights set about restoring *Edirene* as close to her original state as was possible. Booms and sails were fetched from the warehouse up the fjord. The sails were scrapped at once, for they were mouldy and rotten after all those years in store. All stationary and running rigging was renewed throughout, and reserve rolls of sail cloth, coils of rope and wire were brought aboard. The entire bottom was coppered to protect it against the boring creeping things of tropic seas that are capable of turning a newly built boat into a sieve in a few weeks, unless the proper precautions are taken. Then, with a Norwegian skipper and two friends of mine as a volunteer crew, *Edirene* was one day sailed down along the Norwegian Coast to Denmark and into Roskilde fjord.

The following morning work began in earnest. *Edirene* was hauled up on to the same slip in Ericksen and Grøn's yard where, fifteen years previously, the *Monsoon* had been made ready for her long voyage. While carpenters, plumbers and shipwrights worked away with a will the paper held a competition to choose a new name for *Edirene*, one that would be more suitable and romantic. Of the suggestions sent in 1,200 were more or less possible, but the final choice was *Santa Maria*, the name of the ship from whose deck Columbus saw the New World rising out of the sea that October morning in 1492. You see, we, too,

7

were to sail off and discover new worlds, lands that are there plainly marked on the map, but all the same to the general reader just empty names without content or significance because they lie below the horizon of what he is able to survey as he earns his daily bread. We were to see what lay hidden behind some of those names and the *Santa Maria* was to be our means of doing so.

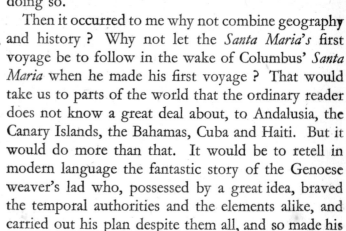

Then it occurred to me why not combine geography and history ? Why not let the *Santa Maria's* first voyage be to follow in the wake of Columbus' *Santa Maria* when he made his first voyage ? That would take us to parts of the world that the ordinary reader does not know a great deal about, to Andalusia, the Canary Islands, the Bahamas, Cuba and Haiti. But it would do more than that. It would be to retell in modern language the fantastic story of the Genoese weaver's lad who, possessed by a great idea, braved the temporal authorities and the elements alike, and carried out his plan despite them all, and so made his name and that of his ship immortal.

Columbus and his ship are linked together as closely as Noah and the Ark. They sail through the dry pages of history with an aureole of glory for the fantastic feat that they accomplished. So, while they hammered and bored and sawed down at the shipyard, I retired .to my desk and began reading up Columbus.

Stacks of heavy tomes appeared on my desk, and, while the spring storms lashed at the branches of the copper beech outside my window, I read them one after the other and not only found them as exciting as any novel, but discovered that during the years

The Author

Columbus has become a figure round which the writers of history have woven a tangled skein of myth and legend, some to glorify him, others to discredit him in the eyes of posterity, some all enthusiasm and no criticism, others all sour criticism and no enthusiasm. As I read I found myself coming to admire Columbus more and more, a real admiration both for the man and for his feat.

One day, after hours of reading, I looked up and saw him standing beside my desk. With one sweep of his hand he brushed all the dusty tomes off my desk. Then he jerked his head in the direction of the window and the storm outside, and said :

" Come ! Hoist sail and follow me. Come and see the horizons that I left, sinking into the sea behind you, and explore the same coasts as I saw rising up in the west.

" Too many books have been written about me by learned folk sitting at their desks. Set sail and stand out across the Atlantic. You are more likely to meet me there than here among the dry leaves of those books."

" Oh ! " said I. " But we must just wait a bit."

" Wait ! " said he, frowning at me as though I were a mutinous sailor in the Sargasso Sea. " Haven't you got your boat ? Haven't you got a big publishing house behind you, as I had Isabella ? If you are finding the same difficulties as I in getting a crew, then go to the governor of your prison and ask him to release a few of his convicts on condition that they sail your boat for you."

" He would never do that," I replied. " Not now that convicts can have weekends off and form their own orchestras, to say nothing of all their other concessions."

"But, any way, it's hardly necessary," I went on, pointing to a pile of 400 letters heaped on my desk. "These are all letters from young men offering to go with me : young men who have been forced to remain inside their country's frontiers during their adolescence because that coincided with the war that has just been waged to ensure us all freedom to the fourth degree. For three years they have waited in vain for freedom to come to the wide world so that they might get to know its other peoples. I only need to pull a few out of the pile and there I have the three men I shall need to follow in the wake of Your Excellency."

"What the devil is the man hesitating for," roared the admiral, looking really angry. "Is it guts he lacks ? Or won't his wife allow it ? "

I looked up at him and shook my head energetically.

"My dear Excellency," said I, "a great deal has happened since your day. Your epoch-making voyage of discovery has led among other things to it being necessary to have a visa if you want to enter any of the countries in the New World. That's one thing with which you didn't have to contend."

A puzzled look came into Columbus' eyes. Then, with a shake of his head he wrapped his purple cape about him and disappeared, leaving a little pool of salt water on the carpet where he had stood.

"Were you talking to someone ? " asked my wife, as she came in with the afternoon coffee.

"Who was it ? " chorused Inger and Jorgen and Ulla.

"Christopher Columbus," I answered, and put the old books back in their places on the bookshelf.

"You have been reading too much again," said my wife.

"Tell us about him," cried the children.

And that's what I shall try to do in the following chapters.

CHAPTER II

We set out

THEY cheered us. The photographers photographed us. We were presented with a ship's bell, bouquets of flowers, and all sorts of other useful and useless gifts. It was all very solemn and impressive, but I couldn't help wondering how many of the people standing there on the quay were thinking, "Well, I suppose that in so-and-so many days we'll see these photos in the papers with the caption 'The last pictures to be taken of the four young men who . . .'"

I was moved, of course, but all the time at the back of my mind was the thought: "Suppose we run aground and wreck the boat and have to wade ashore five or six miles from here ; or suppose we come to blows and have to call off the trip before we have even passed the cliffs of Dover ? What will happen then ? And how many of the gentry standing at the moment rather impressed by our setting out to cross the ocean in such a small boat, won't exult and say "I thought so," and find great delight in the sarcastic remarks the daily papers will pass.

Lose your boat in the Øresund and you're an idiot. But, if you can get across the Atlantic and then run her on a coral reef, that is quite different. That's exciting and interesting, even if you make just as big a hole in her bottom, and even if the wreck in the Øresund was the result of unavoidable circumstances, and that on the coral reef caused by inexcusably bad seaman-ship.

However, there was not a great deal of time for thinking. There were too many people and too many things on deck. The stores weren't yet all stowed; it was beginning to blow up quite a sea out there beyond the jetties, and we had to do all the hundred other things our friends by coming to see us off, had prevented us doing before.

Santa Maria was not a bad little boat now. In fact you would never have recognized the wreck I had first seen in Bergen. We had tipped the two big Wolverine motors overboard. In the first place they were far too powerful for our needs and appallingly expensive to run. Also they had been scandalously neglected. The propeller-shafts hadn't been properly greased and about an inch of the hard metal was worn away. It was a little miracle that we had ever reached Denmark with those two propeller-shafts.

We had done away with the engine-room amidships, and we now had a nice large cabin there instead. Further aft we had installed one of the new Bolinder 40 h.p. diesel engines, which was quite powerful enough for what we needed, which was an auxiliary motor, and, as we were to find, fantastically economical to run, using not much more than a litre of fuel for every knot. Those with a knowledge of such things will know how to appreciate that.

New sails we had. New and larger tanks for water and oil, two tons of each, and another four tanks on deck which could be used for either water or oil as required. These were part of a sort of submarine hide of my own design that I had had made for taking ciné photographs under water along the coral reefs of the Bahamas. Columbus had never thought of that !

There had been no skimping in overhauling the *Santa Maria*. Her equipment was in first class order and we had plenty of provisions. They, in fact, were littered about the deck, in the saloon and in the deck house, and all we had left to do was to get them stowed away so that there might be room for us in our bunks.

And who were we ?

First, there was the skipper, Peter Fribert. He was fifty years old and not quite normal.

Nobody who is fifty and has a perfectly good mate's ticket enabling him to get a job on a steamer any time he likes, those being times when the shipping companies were crying out for navigators, and who instead chooses to sail to and fro across the Atlantic in a 20-metre craft, nobody who does that can be quite normal.

Fribert studied. He also wrote poetry and was a rabid hater of officialdom. He had spent a year in prison in Germany for distributing propaganda leaflets which had not been written by Goebbels, in the streets of Danzig, and that was long before the war started.

Then there was Jens Larsen Underbjerg, our mechanic, bo'sun, ship's carpenter and member of the opposition, aged 33. He was obstinate and reliable, and he knew a whole lot about a great number of things with which one would not expect a fisherman from the west coast of Jutland to be acquainted. With the exception of a visit to Greenland made while in the Navy, he had spent most of his life pulling nets full of plaice and cod into an Esbjerg cutter. He was a specialist on sea birds, and machinery had no secrets from him, at least not after he had pulled the thing to bits and put it together again.

That leaves Niels, Jens' little brother. He, too, had been a fisherman. During the war he took a hand in the work of our Underground, and when he emerged to the surface again, he found that he was in India serving in the British Army. He was with them in Burma and in the Himalayas, and two and a half years later was demobilized as drummer. He was our one and only ordinary seaman, and also our cook.

In Niels' opinion, Escoffier was an old gasbag. He himself abominated tomatoes, salad, and any other food that could be suspected of containing vitamins. And anything he himself did not like, he just would not cook. The only fish he considered fit for human consumption were plaice, eel, herring, mackerel and cod, and I shall never forget his face when once in the Canary Islands I fried a dish of octopus. Never have I seen loathing so obvious and so heartfelt.

Food without potatoes was to him unthinkable, and when for a short time we were forced to make do with sweet potatoes, rice and beans, Niels went on hunger strike. He had the courage of his convictions as far as food was concerned. Yet he was a really good chap with a great fund of humour and imagination.

Niels was also a poet. He wrote lyrics and lampoons with equal facility. He swore like thirty bo'suns just to hide the fact that his mind was as sensitive as a young girl's. He was twenty-seven.

All three were unmarried.

So was Mette. Mette was our ship's cat, a two-month old kitten whom we had met by chance when she was on her way to one of the harbour basins in a sack. We had rescued her from death by drowning, and before long she was playing with a rope's end right for'ard and pretending to be horribly afraid, which she was not.

We stowed and we stowed. All the empty spaces under the bunks and elsewhere were gradually stuffed full. All the things that had looked as though they would have filled a cargo boat, disappeared out of sight and out of our way. It was unbelievable how much a little boat like ours could hold.

The Carlsberg brewery had been very kind and given us 1,000 bottles of different brands as a parting gift. There was porter and lager and pilsner and gold export and Easter brew—all things we had been unable to buy ashore in Denmark since Hitler had planted his flat and booted feet in our garden. Then a kindly man in Antwerp, a real friend of Denmark, got Hellesen's to equip us with our elements, hand lights and morse lamps. He also knew an angelic cigarette manufacturer in Luxembourg who sent us thirty thousand *Amiral* cigarettes of real good pre-war Virginia tobacco, the like of which we had not tasted for several accursed years.

People really had been very kind. In fact, our every desire had been met. When I realized that, it was inevitable that the associated idea should rear its ugly head. That, surely, is what is done for the condemned man in his death-cell ? It was a cheering thought.

There was a place for everything—except the beer.
We had to take the bottles out of their wooden cases
and straw coverings, but still there was nowhere for
them until we hit upon the idea of stuffing them down
through the hatchway and stowing them round the
keel where the frames held them so well that they
never shifted. I should think that was the first time a
ship has put to sea with bottled beer as ballast.

The North Sea was showing its teeth. *Santa Maria*
stamped, as frisky as a schoolgirl. The skipper went
off to the out-hauler boom to reef the spanker. First
Maria dipped her nose in and cocked her stern in the
air. Then she sat back on her tail and ducked the
out-hauler well and truly under; and when I turned
round I saw the skipper's beard a little way below
the surface. A few bubbles were rising from it. Blop,
blop it went, then the skipper was jerked up into the
air again, at the same time as the jib disappeared under
water. He spat a little salt water out to leeward, wrung
out his beard; then he bent forward and doubled up.

Our skipper was seasick. There are some old
sailors who never get over the trial and torment of sea-
sickness. But it seldom lasts more than the first day
or two after leaving every port. Our skipper had been
sailing since Methuselah was a boy and had been
bo'sun on the Ark, but he was seasick all the same.

We sailed down the North Sea and passed the
melancholy avenue of wrecks that marks the way
through Kieler Fjord where large steamers lie on their
sides, like rust-red islands, surrounded by screaming
gulls and visited at rare intervals by a little rowing
boat whose owner hopes to be able to find

something of value that he can wrest from all that former glory.

Evening came. The wind died down as the lights were lit along the docks and quays of Holtenau, and we slid through the Kiel Canal in the dead calm of a summer night from which the clouds had rolled aside to show us a deep black sky strewn with stars. Twisting and turning the canal cut through the country like a broad highway. The two rows of signal lights that fringed it and mirrored themselves in the still, black water of the canal, were like street lamps. Now and again we would slip in and out of a wood, or pass a little house solitary on its dyke, with warm light behind its friendly windows.

The canal was our sally-port into the North Sea, and the North Sea met us with a stiff breeze from the west, heavy seas and mist. And so we crawled on laboriously into the wind. The long chain of the Friesian Islands took an age to disappear astern. Wangeroog, Langeoog, Norderney, Just—it sounds like an incantation. Borkom, Rottum, Schiermonnikoog . . . magic, but not strong enough to bind the wind. It increased from stiff breeze to a full storm from the south-west. Right in our teeth.

Laboriously we beat to windward, each tack seeming only to put us further back. In the end, however, we had worked our way round the corner at Texel and down along the Belgian coast to where Ostend lay blinking its thousands of lights, its big hotels getting ready to close their doors for the winter.

The bulging clouds were crawling slowly across the sky, so low down that they seemed to be wanting to scratch their fat wet stomachs on our mast top. Water was washing in over the forepart and despite our oilskins we were all wet through. Our rubber boots were half-full of water and it took Niels all his time to keep upright in the narrow galley and look after the kettle and the sausages in their frying pan on our two primus stoves.

Jens was almost invisible in the engine room where, in a fog of petrol fumes, carbon monoxide, and oaths, he was trying to persuade our electric light to function. He had been there four hours already and this was his free watch.

None of us had washed or shaved for several days. Talk about carefree voyages and blue lagoons, full moons, deck-chairs and all the etceteras ! Ye gods, at that moment we were off Dunkirk among hundreds of submerged wrecks, in a fairway that had not been properly swept of mines, while the Goodwin Sands were not so very far away. And we were not making any headway. None at all. So we gave up, stuck our tail between our legs and ran for shelter in the lee of the North Foreland.

We dropped anchor in the roads off Margate. Nor were we the first to have had the idea. There were a destroyer, a cable ship, and four steamers already grinding at their anchor chains in the tidal water of the Thames estuary. The wireless was pouring out the most horrifying accounts of storm and floods that had already caused damage worth millions of pounds in England. And overhead whined jet-propelled aeroplanes on test flights. Nice inventions intended to cause still further millions of damage.

19

And meanwhile we played poker and waited for the weather to improve.

CHAPTER III

A Little Further on

DOVER—Brighton—Portsmouth ; but the storm had not meant to abate for good. This was just a slight breathing space of which we had been taking advantage, and now the storm was blowing with increased vigour from the same confounded quarter—the south-west.

"Severe storms are to be expected. There is a gale warning for the western Channel and all Biscay . . ."

The B.B.C.'s announcer was not encouraging.

"What are those islands over there ? " asked Niels, who was taking his turn at the wheel.

"The Channel Islands," I replied. "Casquettes, Alderney, Jersey, Sark and Guernsey."

"What's on them ? " asked Niels again, for he is very inquisitive.

"That I don't know," I admitted. "Nobody has ever been on them."

"Well, it's high time somebody went," said Jens looking pugnacious.

"There would be shelter from the storm," muttered the skipper to Mette and the mizzen mast.

"But not for us !" He went on. "We've got to round Ushant—in this weather. In a south-westerly storm."

"Hard to port ! " I ordered.

That was how we put in to Guernsey, which was quite contrary to our plans, for Guernsey is not a place on which Columbus ever set foot.

In Port St. Peter they thought that we were pirates. We were rather strangely dressed: Jens and Niels like to tie colourful handkerchiefs round their heads, and Niels' upper half is tattooed all over like a present-ation illustrated bible, except that the motives are slightly different. And then there was the skipper's beard. It made him look exactly like the man inside the lifebelt on a packet of Player's cigarettes.

We had ceremonial uniforms with us, but we were reserving them for more exotic landfalls, so it was not till the harbour police had inspected our papers that the pirate myth was finally exploded. They now thought that we were whalers. This was because there were two hand harpoons and a couple of long lances lashed to the starboard shrouds. They were intended to provide us with fresh meat when the dolphins began jumping across our bows—provided any of us were able to hit their shiny backs with them. I don't think, though, that any of us would really have had the heart to do such a thing.

The *Guernsey Evening Post* gave us three columns on the front page and printed a picture of *Maria* and us, and we were all very proud. We liked the island and everything about it, especially the red-haired girl who came down to the quay and smiled at us and bade us welcome.

How many people know that Guernsey and Jersey cheeses and Jersey jerseys and Guernsey sweaters come from some of the most idyllic and charming islands you will find in any European waters ? In their climate, population, and architecture, they are an entrancing mixture of England and the South of

France. Poets have lauded them. Victor Hugo owned a house in Guernsey and it was there that he wrote *Les Miserables* and others of his books. He must often have thought of all the poor wretches who couldn't live on that lovely green island where figs and grapes hang heavily from the branches and ripen alongside tomatoes ; where a sea as clear as crystal washes up over rocks that are red like those of the Riviera, and where so many glories are guarded by mediaeval towers stationed all around the coast.

And how many know that from one point of view, it is the Channel Islands that own England, and not the other way round ?

When William the Conqueror conquered England that time he was Duke of Normandy, and the Channel Islands formed part of his duchy. However, when, after the conquest he decided to settle in England for good, his subjects across the water in Normandy did not like the idea of their duke emigrating and so Normandy broke away. The Channel Islands, however, remained loyal to him, as they have to England ever since. No one can blame them for maintaining contact with the British Empire, which after all is quite a nice and profitable colony for four little islands to possess.

Palms, magnolias and camellias. Black-haired girls whose mentality is a pleasant mixture of the English and French. The Spirit of France lives on in those small islands, which is one of the reasons why they are so fascinating and fabulous. But why should I waste paper describing a few little islands that are outside your own front door ? We had things to do elsewhere.

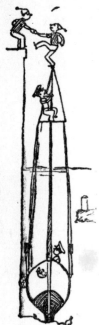

As the storm seemed to have abated, we took the opportunity to have the ship's bottom examined.

There is an interval of ten hours between low and high water in the Channel Islands. That means that you sail comfortably in in the evening, tie up alongside the jetty and go into the town to find your boat when you get back standing high and dry on *terra firma*. The sea has gone out to sea and there isn't a sign of it anywhere in the harbour. Should you have forgotten to slacken your tie ropes, you will find your boat dangling in the air a good way up the wall of the jetty, and all you will be able to do is to hope that the ropes will hold until the tide comes in again.

It was all because it was high water when we came in that Niels was made to look such a fool. He knew perfectly well that in no harbour in the world are you allowed to throw rubbish overboard, and yet he had taken advantage of the dead of night to tip a great deal over the side. Next morning there were six beer bottles, four empty tins that had recently contained tongue and one sardine tin grinning up at him from the dry bottom of the harbour. This being so, Niels had to clamber down and pick all his rubbish up and stow it away neatly on board until we were out at sea again.

Then at last, one morning we heard the voice of the B.B.C. announcer informing us that the storm was abating and there was a prospect of moderate wind and moderate to good visibility in Biscay. That was the way we were going: round Ushant and head first into one of the most feared waterways in the world.

*   *   *

At ebb-tide, Guernsey's old harbour is dry, so you can see the whole boat

Lisbon is a picturesque city and Portugal is a lovely country, but . . .

A good north-easterly breeze took us along the north coast of Normandy and out to the point at Ushant, that dangerous horn that marks the entrance to the world's most unpopular bay in which so many good ships have found their graves. We pulled off our shirts and pretended it was summer. We nodded to the small French fishing-boats and ran alongside one to buy a huge langouste and two lobsters for the price of two packets of cigarettes.

All night lighthouses winked friendlily at us from that rocky coast. The air was mild and warm, and it was not the sort of night to go to bed. I stood in the bows watching *Santa Maria* forging ahead, lifting and pitching, thrilled because at last she had a following wind again. The water curved in two lovely arches on either side of her sharp bows. Every now and again she would heel arrogantly over to leeward and with her gunwale cleave a strip of foam in the dark water that glittered and glinted with phosphorescence. The rigging hummed a gay tune. The everlasting thump of the engine had stopped, and you could hear the blocks creaking. *Santa Maria* swept through the water like a swan : not one of those apathetic birds with clipped wings that live in parks, but one of God's wild birds that with ruffled feathers will attack any-thing or anyone in defence of their young.

And so the night passed.

In the morning great banks of clouds began to gather in the north-west. Slowly and fumblingly they sent out their feelers ; then they began to move, swept low across the sky and extinguished the stars. The seas came rolling at us in great heavy rows, first oily rollers and then topped with foam. The wind moved further and further round, increasing in strength all the time.

The next morning we passed Ushant in a thick drizzle with the wind in the west. It had grown damp and miserable once more and we had again had to resort to our winter clothes. After another day and another night we were lying with reefed sails in the middle of Biscay with the wind against us—back in the south-west.

"Gale warning for Biscay and Finnisterre," said the remarkably unfeeling voice of the B.B.C. announcer, "Severe gales are to be expected." Then there was a click and the voice informed us that light dance music would follow. I threw down the ear-phones and went up on deck to tell the skipper that it was going to begin all over again, only that this time there was no land into the lee of which we could creep for shelter.

And so the storm came. The wind swung between south-west and west, and all the time it increased in strength.

Lower the mainsail. Clew up mizzen and foresail. Clear for storm

And so we lay there, drifting at about two knots. Slowly but surely the wind and the quickly mounting greeny-grey seas were taking us right into the bay.

Course north-west, swinging to east.

At one point in there in the bay the sea bottom suddenly rises steeply and the depth alters from a couple of thousand fathoms to one or two hundred. Against this steep wall the waters raise a cross sea like a maelstrom. But we didn't want to think of that; and anyway there was nothing we could do about it; so we roped the wheel and went below, where we sat and just gazed at each other, while the wireless provided light music. At home, perhaps, they were talking of us, or writing to us that they were with us in spirit, imagining us sitting somewhere in the shade of palms eating bananas from the huge bunches that dangled among the large leaves above our heads.

It was not always easy to know which way up things were supposed to be. At any rate, it was strange to see a paraffin lamp burning at an angle of 45 degrees. And an endless succession of roaring waves came tumbling in from the Atlantic, each dealing *Santa Maria* a blow on the snout as it passed, until her every plank creaked and groaned. She subsided beneath their weight, but each time she bravely got up again and straightened herself to receive the next blow. And all the time we were being driven slowly to the north-west, into the bay.

There was no sleep for us; partly because of the magnificence of the spectacle and of the howling of the wind, and partly because we were flung from side to side of our bunks and had to hang on tight, braced between the wall and the edging board, if we were to avoid being thrown out. And the continual motion up and down and to the side created a sort of seething vacuum in our heads, made our ears sing and rendered all serious thought impossible. We became drowsy, our heads fell forward—and then the boat would be shaken by another thundering blow and for a moment she would stand quite still as though paralysed, then dip forward into the trough, while the water poured foaming across her deck and raced backwards and forwards till it found its way out at last through the scuppers.

There was nothing else for us to do but to sit there and gaze at each other, or to fish out a pack of cards. We ate such food as it was possible to cook in a frying pan that one moment was the right way up, upside down the next, and then lying on its side. The sou'-wester seemed determined to teach us to respect it, before it let us go.

In the end the happy moment came, when, after putting on the earphones to hear what the weather was to be for the next twenty-four hours and impatiently listening to the forecast of conditions round Iceland, in the Channel and the Bight of Heligoland we heard a voice that suddenly sounded angelic, telling us that Biscay could count on a moderate to fresh wind from the north-west with occasional showers and moderate to good visibility. After that we forgot and forgave everything and went on deck to make all clear and to continue our voyage in the right direction.

Slowly the seas abated, gradually the great waves turned into broad rollers. The mainsail was set, at first with a couple of reefs, and so *Santa Maria* turned back on her course, rolling and pitching still, but gradually settling into a quiet sober pace that sent the red and white strokes of the log chasing each other as the pointer moved across the scale recording mile after mile at shorter and shorter intervals.

Our next landfall was Cape Ortegal, a good way east of Finisterre. The storm had driven us far too far in, but it was good for our eyes to see the Spanish coast. Astern, there were still big, louring banks of cloud over Biscay.

We rounded the corner at Cape Vilano and Finisterre, where the Portuguese Norther awaited us. Soft and pleasant, it blew across the deck, made our flag flutter and filled the mainsail that had not a single reef in it for the first time since leaving the Kiel Canal. Jib and foresail were filled and taut. The spanker drew its share of the load, and so with a gentle breeze astern we ran along the coast at seven knots, on past Vigo and the other towns of North Spain till we came to the mouth of the Rio Minho and passed the dividing line between Spain and Portugal.

We had reckoned on being there fourteen days earlier, but the sou'wester had proved us optimists. However, there was a new country smiling friendlily at us. We could forget such things as dates and time-tables.

We edged close in to within half a mile of the coast  and followed it so. It was a clear-cut coastline rising steeply from a sandy beach, and there were no treacherous submerged rocks to make it unsafe to go in close. Town after town slipped past, little fishing towns most of them, but there were larger ones with a cathedral crowned by two towers and large holiday hotels. The coast was an almost unbroken line of white beach. Only here and there would there be a rocky point jutting out into the sea, the last outpost of some chain of mountains inland.

That evening there was a full moon that made sailing sheer delight. Biscay and the North Sea were forgotten, forgotten the wreck-buoys and marked channels to which ships were forced to keep, here we were on a sea that had never been contaminated by magnetic mines, where all could sail freely wherever they wished, provided only that they took care to see that there was enough water under the keel. And in the morning, when the mist was clearing off the sea, we saw queer boats emerging out of the retreating coils, long narrow craft with pointed bows and an elongated stern such as the boats of the old Vikings had. They came towards us across the glittering sea rowed by eight pairs of oars, like strange relics of the galleys of olden times.

These were the local fishing boats either setting out, or making their way home, their owners poor industrious men who had either no knowledge of, or no use for, the modern accessories that would have lightened their task, the people who supply the fat sardines that grace the hors d'oeuvres tray of every luxury restaurant. At night we glimpsed them as vague shadows in a strip of moonlight. They carried no lights, but if they thought a steamer was coming dangerously close they would light a fluttering flare made of bits of rag, or just simply strike a whole box of matches. It does occasionally happen that the crew of a boat will fall asleep and their fragile craft be cut in two by the sharp bows of some great speeding steamer. Sometimes the look-out will notice what has happened, but often the man high up on the bridge remains unaware of the accident, unless there is a piece of a torn sail found on the steamer's anchor when she next puts in to port.

We waved good morning to every fishing boat we passed and to the big four-masted schooners in the roads outside Figueira. Then we passed Nazaré where large fir woods creep inquisitively down to the shore and whisper with the sea. All along the coast were hundreds of windmills perched on top of the cliffs, the characteristic windmills against which Don Quixote tilted, round stone towers with sails like four balaleikas joined by the neck.

That was real holiday sailing, and it made us wish for music. Not till then did we discover that we didn't have a single musical instrument on board, so we decided to put in to Lisbon and buy an accordion.

CHAPTER IV

Lisbon

IT may well be that there are plenty of accordions to be had in Lisbon. I am even ready to believe that they make magnificient ones and decorate them with the same garlands of flowers and song-birds as they paint on the sterns of their little boats, so that even an ordinary coal barge is gay with decoration. That may well be, but I cannot state it as a fact.

There is something very attractive about Lisbon. The inhabitants twitter rather than talk. The fish-wives who gather every morning in the gaily coloured covered market and down by the quay where the fishing boats tie up, are themselves gaily clad in blouse and colourful skirt. They have long black shawls draped over their heads on top of which is a sort of doughnut like those acrobats use when one has to stand on another's head. On top of this is the woven basket in which they carry the fish. They never seem to touch the basket with their hands, but rather keep them for gesticulation. And their gestures are so expressive that I cannot see why the Portuguese ever bothered to acquire a spoken language. When they speak, the twitter of bird-like noises that pours from their mouths, just seems to be reiterating what they have already said in the language of the deaf and dumb.

I will even go so far as to admit that the accordions they make in Lisbon may have a lovely tone, for the

and brilliant smiles

In Andalusia there are shady streets

Portuguese are a very musical people—only I was never able to buy one.

One day when Portugal shall have a different government, fewer policemen, and a little system in the labyrinth of corridors you have to traverse before you can get your papers in order, I shall go back to Lisbon and see if I cannot get one of their accordions with painted garlands of flowers and song-birds, and a lovely soft tone. Also, I should have liked to have seen a little more of Lisbon and the home of port wine than I was able to do in my wanderings from office to office with the Danish Consul's broad back in front to guide me through the twisting streets and intricate systems of corridors.

Poor, industrious, tireless, helpful Beckmann! What he and the whole Danish Legation went through during our short stay in that city on the Tejo; well, you could write an epic about it. Instead, I shall have to send them this book as a thanks-offering for all their help. It wasn't their fault that Portugal hates all tourists and especially people who write and take photographs.

There was a time when I thought I would like to write a whole book about Portugal, home of sardines, corks and wine. That was just after the second world war. I sent an application for a visa to the Portuguese consul in Copenhagen and attached to it every letter of recommendation that I could lay hands on. For six months I heard nothing. Then I asked a good friend in our legation in Lisbon to give me his help. He intervened on my behalf in both high circles and low. The Danish Foreign Office gave me its support. But all the time the official on whose decision the granting of my visa depended was either on leave, on a duty journey, or away ill. And I still haven't received a reply to my application.

Sailors do not require to have visas, and I had thought that I should be able to sneak ashore as a sailor and get a deal of copy about Portugal while *Santa Maria* lay in Lisbon. But in Portugal sailors have to exchange their passports against a yellow ticket when they go ashore. Their passports are deposited at the police station as long as their ship is in. When the harbour police came out in their boat, they told us that the international police would come out immediately we had anchored and give us yellow passes in exchange for our passports. We waited patiently for seven hours, but not a policeman did we see. Then I decided to brave death, the Devil and the Portuguese prison system and go ashore and pay the Danish consul a visit. I went.

The consul went to work at once. We walked miles of dark corridor, from girl to girl, only to be told—when the young ladies had finished discussing their private affairs—that we were in the wrong building and must go to another street and down more long corridors. From there we would be sent to another building in yet another street. All our time in Lisbon I spent tramping from office to office and saw nothing but steps, corridors and dark waiting-rooms.

The trouble was that I had had the unfortunate idea of showing a film about Denmark that I had on board to the Danish colony in Lisbon. To show a film in Portugal to-day is a risky undertaking comparable to driving a lorry loaded with nitro-glycerine through the main streets of Lisbon. First, you require permission to show the film. Having got that, you require a permit to bring the film itself ashore. Then, you must make a written application to yet a third department for a written permit to institute a gathering of more than five persons, while the owner of the hall or building in which the gathering is to be held must also have a permit from the police allowing its use for that purpose.

Each permit has to be fetched from a different department and building. We trudged up and down many, many streets. Now and again I would catch a glimpse of a lovely picturesque town, an old castle, and smiling happy people who apparently all had their papers in order, but then the gloomy corridors would close in upon me again. My feet grew sore from the mosaic paving of the streets, and my behind began to ache from so much sitting on hard wooden benches. I became one of the regulars and soon was nodding to the small grey men who sat on the benches day after day looking as though they had abandoned all hope.

We appealed for help to the legation. Letters were written and calls paid upon high officials, and in the end all was in order. Invitations were sent out to the members of the colony and people began to arrive, many from the country districts. But then it appeared that we still lacked a paper, the permit from the Customs which we had to have before we could be allowed to take the film itself ashore; but the Director of Customs who could have issued it in a trice was on his way to America. We offered to let an armed customs officer accompany us and stay with the film until it was taken back on board. They would not hear of that. The Danish Minister intervened in person; but nothing helped. The film remained on board, and those we had invited had to go back home without seeing it. They took it very nicely, but, of course, they were accustomed to life in Portugal. I was not, and that is the sort of thing I cannot stomach. When you go ashore the place is swarming with police. They are thick along the quays. You can see their grey uniforms on every pavement and by every cafe. They even sail about the harbour in boats, girded with patent-leather belts and impressively large revolvers. There are police with black caps, others with green caps, and the cream of the lot wear green shirts, which are unpleasantly reminiscent of a period one would prefer to forget. Also, or so the people of Lisbon say, the plain clothes police number as many again. They are the ones who walk about keeping an eye on you and seeing that you don't pull a hand grenade out of your pocket and begin fiddling with its mechanism. And then there is yet another department whose officers keep an eye on the other police to see that they are keeping an eye on you.

The next morning I gave up the struggle.

I wanted to get away from Lisbon just as quickly as I could, so taking the patient consul with me I went straight to the office where we had deposited our passports when we were given our yellow passes. I wanted those passports back again. But don't think that I could get them just like that.

There I was with the four yellow passes in my hand, and there was the Danish Consul standing beside me as my guarantor; but it was not a thing that could be done so easily. We were told that a policeman would have to go back on board with us and hand us our passports individually *there*. Unfortunately, for the moment, they didn't have a policeman they could send. We waited three-quarters of an hour for one. That was the time it took him to finish his conversation and his afternoon coffee. Then he wouldn't trust himself to the rubber dinghy we used for such purposes, and we were forced to hire a motor-boat that was as large as *Santa Maria* herself to take him out. That cost 30/- in hard Portuguese money.

The policeman went aboard. He received our yellow passes and we our passports, and he stamped everything umpteen times. The moment he had put the last stamp on the last passport, I gave the order to get under weigh, and before he and our good angel, the consul, had scrambled over the rail down into their large luxurious motor-boat, our own engine had been started and we began to move.

But we never got our accordion.

During the four days that I had spent wandering from office to office, I had at least got an occasional glimpse of a city that was beautiful and charming, golden with sunlight and lovely. And so we sailed away down the Tejo past the magnificent villas on the shore, and past Belem Tower which saw the start of so many voyages of discovery in the old days of Henry the Navigator, Vasco da Gama and Magellan.

Columbus, too, first tried his luck in Portugal; for it was while he was working as a draughtsman in Lisbon drawing sea-charts, that he conceived the idea that led to his discovery of America. He, too, was a foreigner in that city on the Tejo, and he too ran his head against officialdom and wore out his shoes tramping dark corridors. He, too, came up against the same endless rows of dusky little men who could see the sense of what he proposed, but, they were sorry—so sorry that they turned up their eyes, raised their hands aloft, shrugged their shoulders and smiled most charmingly—they could not decide, that was a matter for those higher up. And those higher up are never in their offices.

I can well understand how Columbus gradually grew footsore and despondent. Had I been he, I too would have shaken the dust of Lisbon from my shoes and gone to Spain to ask Ferdinand and Isabella if they would like a present of South, Central, and North America. Luckily they said yes, and that is why to-day we have Rita Hayworth, bubble gum, Ford motor cars, and tobacco (life would not have been easy if we had had to do without the last named). So, we, who were following in Columbus' wake sailed in our turn southwards for Spain to put *Santa Maria*, the skipper's beard, Mette, Niels, Jens and myself, to say nothing of our boundless thirst for discovery, at the service of that country. And we discovered that we were welcome.

The key which opened Spain to us was the name Christopher Columbus. We discovered that as soon as we took the pilot aboard outside the dangerous sand-

banks that restrict all traffic for the rivers Odiel and
Tinto. These two rivers flow into each other a few
sea miles from the bar. On the Odiel is the port of
Huelva, known and busy shipping port for cork and
for the ore from the Rio Tinto mines, and a little way
up the Rio Tinto is a little country township, Palos
de Maguer, that to-day is quite unknown, but five
hundred years ago it was a large and important sea-
port. Now, it lies well inland behind a tall fold in the
ground. You cannot even see it from the river, and
the river itself is silted up and all traffic stopped. All
the same, it is one of those places where world history
was made, for it was from there that Columbus set out
with his three ships on that memorable 3rd August,
1492.

To-day Columbus is as well-loved and popular in
Spain as Tordenskjold in Denmark, Robin Hood in
England, and Ingrid Bergman in the U.S.A.
Sufficient of the spirit of the Conquistadores still lives
on in Spanish hearts for their dark eyes to light up the
moment they heard that men from the North were on
their way to follow the wake that had been the
foundation of Spain's centuries of greatness. All the
same, Spain seems to have forgotten Palos.

Huelva with its quays and cranes and far greater
population has deprived Palos of its power and in-
fluence. Palos, behind its ridge, is a bare mile and a
half from Huelva as the crow flies, yet no one in that
port seemed to know for certain whether or not there
was a post office at Palos.

The two towns are on opposite sides of the river,
but to get from Huelva to Palos by road you must

drive twenty miles inland before you come to a bridge which will take you across. It is far easier to get from Huelva to the monastery of Rabida, which stands where the two rivers meet. That is the road all tourists take.

Rabida Monastery is where on 12th October of every year is celebrated the anniversary of Columbus' landing in San Salvador. The representatives of all the South and Central America States come pouring in for the occasion. Spanish and South American warships anchor in the river and fire salutes. Speeches are made and masses sung, but Palos lies forgotten behind its steep slopes and poor vineyards. Palos has quite given up the sea and fairy-tale adventure.

Come to Rabida ! The Monastery where Columbus stayed. Rabida, from which Columbus started on his epoch-making voyage !

Rabida—Rabida—Rabida ! I was beginning to get pretty sick of the sound of Rabida. Why couldn't they let Palos into the picture ?

No matter with whom I talked, whether it was the pilot or the ferryman who takes the tourists from the bus across to the monastery, they were all unanimous that it would be quite impossible for a boat of *Santa Maria's* draught to get up the Rio Tinto and anchor off Palos. There wasn't nearly enough water, they told us. We would find ourselves stuck on a mudbank, before we were halfway. And anyway, they asked, why did we want to go to that hole? Rabida was the place.

Rabida ! Rabida ! ! Rabida ! ! !

All those who had never been there said that there was nothing to see in Palos. And the more people told me that, the more necessary it became for me to go there. I *wanted* to start from Palos. I wanted to weigh anchor at exactly the same point in the river as that where Columbus had given the order to hoist sail.

We anchored where the pilot showed us off the fine jetty at Rabida. He would take us no farther up the Rio Tinto, but I swore that we should get to Palos —with the boat and all. For the time being, however, we let the pilot go ashore comforted by the thought that we had quite given up that impracticable idea. When he had gone, we ourselves followed to have a look at the monastery, like any other tourists.

CHAPTER V

Rabida

THE monastery of Rabida lies on a steep slope at the confluence of the rivers Tinto and Odiel. The hill on which it was built hundreds of years ago rises out of flat water meadows and is covered with a confusion of geranium bushes with blood-red flowers, large agaves and slender date palms, with the occasional pool of flame of some bougainvillæas as a relief to so much greenery. Up the trunks of the trees winds bindweed with flowers as large as roses and as redly blue as violets.

The monastery has white walls and a roof of red tiles, above which a belfry just protrudes. In it hangs the self-same bell that was ringing for Mass when Columbus' three caravels slipped down on the ebb-tide four and a half centuries ago. On the low point, between the monastery and the river, there is now a large cannery with a number of low buildings and jetties to which the fishing boats bring their cargoes of sardines and tunny-fish from the seas between Cape St. Vincent and Gibraltar. Otherwise there has not been much visible change since that August morning in the year 1492.

As might have been expected, a pillar topped with a globe and a cross has been set up in memory of the event, and of course a real spider's web of legend has been woven about Rabida until the old monastery has become a place of pilgrimage to which tourists have flocked in such numbers that the Franciscan monks have had to leave it and seek elsewhere the peace they need for prayer and meditation. Only four brethren remain there, and they it is who take visitors round that sacred spot.

This is the legend of Columbus.

He left Portugal for Spain after the Court at Lisbon  had lost patience with his cranky idea that there was a shorter way to the rich lands of India than that round the Cape of Good Hope, or the arduous overland route from the east coast of the Mediterranean through Syria and Arabia to India, Japan and China. There were so many came to Lisbon wanting to go off and discover fresh golden lands, and one and all were ready to guarantee that they would return with treasure galore could they but have a few ships, the crews, and a good advance in cash. The Court was as overrun with them as is the office of a large newspaper today with young men wanting to bicycle to Cape Town, or to go round the world on a scooter. Columbus was just one of many, and nobody would listen to him and his ideas.

The Genoese cartographer was offended and went to Spain in a huff. Spain was slightly envious of Portugal which had established itself along the coast of Africa and was making a lot of money by trading and plundering in the Far East. But Spain had been involved in a long protacted war with the Moors who had overrun the country, and it was not till they had been forced back to North Africa, whence they had come, that the Spaniards had either the time or the money for colonial conquest. Of course they did already have one or two colonies. They had, for example, a firm footing in the Canary Islands, most of which they had pacified, though the main island of Teneriffe was still putting up a stout resistance. Even on the other islands the governors had to be constantly on the watch lest the warlike natives, the Guanchoes, should rise against them.

The war with the Moors had left Spain with little money for expensive expeditions into the unknown, and to begin with Columbus had great difficulty in obtaining audience with King Ferdinand and Queen Isabella. The Chancellor of the Exchequer would not hear of his proposal, and much preferred the counsels of caution of those who shared the Portuguese opinion of Columbus as an adventurer and dreamer. In the end Columbus grew tired of running his head against blank walls and decided that he would go to France and take his thirteen-year-old son, Diego, with him.

So it was that one day the two came tired, thirsty and hungry to the little monastery of Rabida and hammered on its door to ask for bread and water. The gentle brothers saw to their needs, fetching cool water for them from the monastery well, and as they ate listened to the elder traveller's account of his disappointments. The tale was repeated to the abbot, Juan Perez. It intrigued him and he sent for Columbus, and at the same time invited the physician in Palos, Garcia Fernandez, to come and hear what he would have to say.

So eloquent and persuasive was Columbus, so convincing were the maps he produced, that the wise abbot who had once been Queen Isabella's confessor, begged him not to leave the country until he had been able to discuss the matter more thoroughly with the queen. Meanwhile Columbus was to be the guest of the monastery. And then the miracle happened. After the wise and pious abbot had spoken with the queen, she changed her mind : Columbus was recalled to Madrid, given his ships and crews and equipment, and in return Spain received all South and Central America along with all the treasure the Spaniards were able to carry away.

It is a nice legend and one that is most flattering to the Catholic Church ; but unfortunately it is only a legend with a very flimsy basis.

Whatever the truth, there is nothing in the archives to indicate that Rabida monastery had any hand in the affair, except that an abbot, Juan Perez, sat on the committee which was to help Columbus get his equipment, and which also had the delicate task of deciding what titles, cash and emoluments he was to receive, were he to come back with a whole new world for the Spanish crown. And anyway what was that disappointed would-be discoverer doing on the desolate promontory on which the monastery lies, when he was supposed to be on his way from Granada to France ? One look at the map is sufficient to see what a pointless detour that would have been. France lies to the north-east of Granada, and Rabida to the south-west. And even if it hadn't been pointless, if Columbus had been intending to take ship from one of the southern ports, such as, for example, Palos which in those days was quite well-known, Palos is still three miles from Rabida. And at Rabida the road ends, and the land peters out in a sandy, marshy promontory. What on earth could have taken Columbus and his son out there?

And how is it that Queen Isabella's father confessor was ending his days in one of the smallest and poorest monasteries in Spain, miles away from the royal residence? If the abbot had in fact been the queen's confessor, then to send him to that poor monastery in its desolate surroundings could only have meant one thing, degradation, and in that event it is unthinkable that the queen would have let herself be over-persuaded by the man she had degraded.

No, we shall be closer to the historical and less romantic truth, if we assume that all that happened was that with the end of the Moorish war the court found that it had the time and the money to indulge in the colonial experiments which had so long attracted it. Columbus happened to be on the spot, and he got the job.

If we stick to the dry historic facts, we shall be fairly safe in saying that Columbus met the abbot of Rabida for the first time the day he came to Palos having in his pocket a document signed by Ferdinand and Isabella calling upon the burghers of that town to equip three ships for a voyage of discovery to the west. There is no telling whether he ever visited the monastery, but it was certainly not till all his arrangements had been made and he was ready to sail, and possibly not till the actual morning of his departure. However, that has not prevented the Franciscans from building him a temple there on the end of that tongue of land where the two rivers meet. And they have been so clever that no one now thinks of Palos, three miles away, for all that it is the historic starting-point of his voyage and its church the one in which he prayed before he raised anchor and set sail.

One of the four monks will show you the very gateway through which Columbus passed after his son had slaked his thirst with water from the well. " There it is, ladies and gentlemen, just as you see it there." And then he will reverently point out the altar with its ivory madonna set against a background of silver rays before which Columbus knelt in prayer before he started, or so they will tell you. There are always thick wax candles burning in front of that madonna and glinting on her lips whose gentle smile is as enigmatic as that of the Mona Lisa. After that you will be taken to the first floor and into a large room whose windows look out over the river. See, there at the foot of the slope is where Columbus' ships lay and took water on board, while the abbot blessed Columbus, who kissed his hand before going back to his caravels and giving the order to hoist sail. Here in this room Columbus is supposed to have explained his plan to the abbot and to the doctor from Palos. Models of his ships are there, each in its glass case. There are cupboards in which lie flags like those that fluttered from the tops of the three masts. One whole wall is taken up by a colourful map showing Columbus' route, and the main events of the voyage are depicted in four huge paintings. As far as one can judge these must have been painted half, or three-quarters of a century ago. In them you can find those

very rooms, the self-same gateway, the same view, all exact down to the slightest detail, just as the brothers show them to-day to the tourists who come to render Columbus homage. There you are, that proves it ! You can recognize it all in these old paintings. . . .

Sancta simplicitas . . . but all the same Columbus has been stolen from that modest little town of Palos, where the events really took place.

I photographed everything and everybody, as was expected of me ; and there were some nice subjects, peaceful cloisters with red flowers, and a solitary black cat washing its paws in the sunshine on the old paving stones. I photographed them all to the evident delight of the beaming Franciscan brother at my side, or was that due to the excellence of the Virginia cigarette I had thrust into his mouth in an attempt to stem his loquacity ? Then I went back on board to find that meanwhile we had been honoured with a visit from two distinguished gentlemen.

One introduced himself as the mayor of Palos, the other as the chief of that town's police. They explained that they had read about us in the Huelva newspaper and then seen us anchor here off Rabida. They had now come to ask—with all politeness— whether we were not intending to start from Palos. Columbus, they informed us, had started from Palos and a voyage in his wake would be nonsensical if we did not begin it at the same point as he. So I told them that I knew Columbus had started from Palos and that from the very beginning I had intended to follow exactly in his wake, doing the same as he, but that the harbourmaster, the customs officials, the ships' agent,

the pilot and all the ragtag and bobtail on Rabida quay
had been at great pains to tell us that there was far too
little water up the river for a ship of our size to go any
farther.

"You shall start from Palos," said the mayor.

The chief of police nodded agreement, so that the
sun danced across his black, three-cornered helmet.

"That's all very well," said I. "But we don't want
to run her aground."

"Do you trust me?" asked the mayor.

I looked him up and down: a small, rather skinny
man with a good-looking face and a very energetic
turn to the corners of his mouth and to the jut of his
chin, nose long and regular, his gaze steady.

"Yes," said I.

"Do you trust the chief of police?" asked the
mayor again.

I took one look at the high representative of authority and gave a hasty affirmative bow in his direction.

"Then start up your motor, cast off, and just
follow my directions."

And that is what we did.

With the mayor as our pilot, and the town's chief
of police as hostage for the accuracy of his directions,
we slipped away from Rabida jetty and out into the
Rio Tinto. Half an hour later we had arrived and had
the Palos jetty right to starboard. And we hadn't
touched bottom once.

We took a sounding. There was plenty of water
and soft mud on the bottom.

"Let go the anchor," said I.

That is how we arrived at Palos.

CHAPTER VI

Palos

Our clattering anchor found bottom in the deep red mud of the Rio Tinto. *Santa Maria* swung in the current for a moment and came to rest with her bows pointing towards the sea. The incoming tide gurgled coolly along her white sides. We had arrived.

Our anchor lay in exactly the same spot, where Columbus had anchored his three caravels more than four and a half centuries before. He had lain there to take the last of his gear aboard before setting out for where reality came to an end and fantasy and imagination ran riot.

A broad stream flowing between low sun-scorched slopes : Rio Tinto. To the south, behind the gentle rise of the slope we could just glimpse the roofs of a small town, a few white walls, a church, and leading from them, a narrow road that came twisting and turning down to the river and the primitive jetty off which we lay. So that was Palos.

Four or five hundred years ago Palos had been a town of some importance, but now. . . . We straightened our backs and looked towards it. Then we looked at each other : "Well, here we are." There had been moments when we had almost begun to doubt whether we would ever get there, but those were now past and forgotten, forgotten as Palos has been all these years since Columbus and his company of crazy men set tongues wagging in that remote Andalusian township. To-day it is but a name in the history books, five letters hooked on to Columbus' feat.

It might just as easily have been Cadiz or Seville, or Porto Santa Maria, but chance willed it that it was the good people of Palos who had somehow or other offended and incurred the wrath of the mighty king of Spain. They had to do penance for their sins, material penance which involved providing a Genoese adventurer with three well-found caravels and suitable crews to engage in the fantastic undertaking of sailing to the rim of the world and on into the dreaded fiery chasm, if that was what they should find there.

The men of Palos were by no means the worst who could have been found for the job. They were seamen. And in those days sailors did not just sail coal from Newcastle to Struer, or dried cod from Iceland to Spain. They had to be able to turn a hand to most things. If there were no freights to be got in the Mediterranean, if the market was dull in the Levant, well they turned to piracy for a while, and if there weren't many enemy ships about, a fellow countryman with a full load did very well instead. If I am not greatly mistaken the men of Palos had been indulging in a little piracy and that was why they had incurred the wrath of Isabella and Ferdinand. They had been tempted into attacking a Spanish boat. And so, one day, there was Columbus standing in the church of Palos holding a letter from the king in his hand. As the councillors and burghers listened to him

reading it out, their faces must have grown longer and longer. They had not bargained for this.

That was 23rd May, 1492.

The men of Palos growled and grumbled. This was too much. They had no intention of following a mad foreigner to the end of the world. Tension grew, until it looked as though they might in the end revolt, and the castle that dominates the town from its eminence near the church was put in a state of defence. In the middle of this grim situation Martin Alonzo Pinzon returned home from a voyage to the Mediterranean coast. Naturally, one of the first things he heard was an indignant account of Columbus and his mission, but his fellow townsmen got no sympathy from him. Instead, he told them he thought they were mad. Freights were falling; there were few Portuguese prizes to be had, and they knew what sort of a fuss there was when they nabbed a Spanish boat. Altogether things were pretty dull now that the Moors had been turned out of the country, and here was this excellent Genoese, come with the whole court behind him, telling them that he was dead sure that there was a much shorter way to India than that round the southern end of Africa which so far everyone had been using, and yet they didn't want to go with him ! Didn't they realize that, if they could find that route, it would mean that they would be able to bring cargoes of spices and silks back to Palos quicker than had been possible before ? Palos would be in right at the very beginning. His advice to them was that they should sign on the dotted line, pack their sea-chests and get aboard as fast as they could. That at

any rate was what he was going to do and his young
brother with him. And success would also bring them
back into favour with Ferdinand and Isabella and
make them forget the unfortunate little episode to
which they owed the presence of Columbus in their
town.

After that popular opinion swung right round.
If Don Martin spoke well of a thing, then it must be
all right. He was one of them, had worked his way
up till he occupied a leading position in Spanish shipping, and he was known as a good navigator and a
bold seaman.

That, then, was how Columbus got his three ships
and the hundred men to man them, and why he
started his daring voyage from the port of Palos on
the Rio Tinto.

To-day, Palos is but a little white town on a hillside
above the river. Its streets are dead, its inhabitants few,
and they have turned their backs on the sea. Nowadays, in the blazing sunshine of Andalusia they sweat
behind primitive wooden ploughs such as the Romans
used. They grow tomatoes, hoe their potatoes, and
harvest a few grapes which they turn into a wine of
no renown, just a few barrels for their own use.

A little boat came out to us. It had one of those
lovely lateen sails which keep their beauty of line
even though they are so torn and ragged that they
hardly hold together. In her, leaning against the mast,
stood a woman in her thirties, dressed in black as
poor women always are in Spain. She was pale-faced
and sad, but she was a direct descendant of Martin
Alonzo Pinzon and had come out just to have a look

at us who sailed in a ship that was called *Santa Maria* and had announced their intention of crossing the Atlantic in the wake of her ancestors.

Up in Palos' market place there is a dazzling white marble statue of Pinzon. On the outside wall of the church there is a plaque in memory of the two brothers' feat, and another inside with the names of those who were mayor and incumbent during the four hundred years before the discovery of America. But nowhere in Palos did I see Columbus' likeness, not even his name. In the churchyard there was a pillar on which had been engraved the text of the royal command to the burghers of Palos. That was all.

The grounds dips steeply away from the church down to a triangular field where they now grow maize. In those old days the river came in here and formed a shallow bay, across which the ungainly ship's boats of the *Santa Maria* were rowed when they came to fill their large wooden casks with fresh spring water. The well from which they fetched it is still there. It was already old in Columbus' time, for the Romans had built it in those distant days when their eagles were still firmly established in the Iberian Peninsula. But now it is dry. The aqueduct which brought the water from the hills to the covered stone-built well was broken long ago. Its only practical use nowadays is as a lavatory for those using the highway in and out of Palos.

And the church is still as it was. The pulpit is the same, the altar the same, the decorations the same. Nothing has changed since the day Columbus read out the royal command in front of the assembled burghers.

I am not religious, but I must admit that I felt a thrill, a sort of lump in my throat, when the alcalde took me to Mass the first Sunday we lay off Palos. We all sat in an ancient box-pew: the alcalde, the chief of police, the commander of the fort on the coast, the head of the fire brigade, and all the other dignitaries. While the priest performed his monotonous rites, the children in front pinched each other in the behind, tittered, and flicked paper pellets at each other's heads. The town's dogs wandered in and out unconcernedly sniffing and lifting their legs against the massive grey pillars of the church; the mayor hawked and spat on the stone floor; a solitary choir boy tinkled his silver bell every now and again in the half darkness round the altar; and I sat there with my thoughts far away from it all, in fact four and a half centuries away.

The atmosphere of those distant days came oozing out from the dark corners of the church, obliterating the happenings of the moment, and my imagination filled the empty pulpit with a man of about my own age, who was consumed with a burning faith in his idea. In his two hands he held a royal command. There was nothing monotonous about his voice. The fanaticism of a mature man gave it resonance. And there in front of him sat the burghers of Palos, their faces sour and motionless, but reflecting a latent aversion that grew stronger and stronger when they had left the church and begun to discuss the affair in the strong sunshine outside.

Palos was the starting-point for an undertaking that brought about a fantastic revolution in the economy of the world and in the balance between the great powers. In the little grey church of this remote Spanish town was laid the foundation stone of the mighty empire of Spain that was to include all Central and South America until it became poisoned from within by insatiable greed and crashed in ruins three hundred years later. But, all the same, Columbus' name is scarcely ever mentioned there to-day.

" Who after all was Columbus," said the alcalde. " A mystic Italian of whose origins not much is known. He came here with a crazy idea—but it was Martin Alonzo Pinzon who took it up, got him his crews and brought the voyage to a successful conclusion. Martin was the seaman, the navigator—and it is due to him that America was discovered."

You see, Palos and its alcalde consider that Martin Alonzo Pinzon was the true discoverer of America, and that is why there is a marble statue of him in front of the " Bar Pinzon ", which belongs to the alcalde, and why on its well-stocked shelves there are innumerable bottles of " Anis Pinzon ", and why the descendants of the Pinzons came out to greet the *Santa Maria*.

The mumble of the last mass died away up by the altar, where two dejected candles were fighting a vain battle with the darkness. The priest and the choir-boy bent their knees, a dog was kicked out through the door, and the mass was over. We blinked as we came out into the sunlight, greeted the señoras and señoritas as they modestly set off for home, their black hair draped with the lacework of their mantillas. Then all the menfolk collected in the Bar Pinzon for an *aquardiente* or an anis. The chief of the fire brigade was there, and the captain from the fort, an air force lieutenant on leave, and of course the alcalde, who stood drinks all round, and as soon as he had changed we were joined by the priest. The leading wine manufacturer in the town came and sat at our table, and afterwards we went across the street to see his large enclosed yard into which cart after cart kept coming in from the vineyards groaning under heavy loads of golden-green grapes which were tipped out on to a cement floor, from which two dark-eyed men with bare feet shovelled them into a rusty mill that ground all the juice out of them. A turgid grey-green fluid poured out of this wine-press and washed across the cement floor, over the men's black toes and my freshly-cleaned shoes to disappear down a hole in the ground into a pipe which led it across the yard and into large casks in a huge cellar, where it was left to ferment.

We tasted the finished product, young wine from Palos, golden like sunshine, as sweet as the nectar of flowers, rich and full-bodied. I should imagine Columbus took a cask or two with him on his voyage.

The next morning, when Niels, Jens and I walked across the rickety wooden bridge that constitutes Palos' harbour and went ashore, we were saluted by a member of the Guardia Civil. Those who wear the varnished three-cornered helmets of the Guardia Civil have a most delightful form of salutation : they lay their right hands on their hearts. The one who thus greeted us never so much as looked at my camera and the rest of my photographic equipment which make me look like a pack-donkey whenever I go ashore. I returned his salutation with a gracious nod and thought of Lisbon.

A boy was standing at the end of the jetty. He followed us, and the four of us walked on towards Palos, three-quarters of a mile away at the end of a level stretch of road running through water meadows. On it we met other laden donkeys, creaking carts and old women with heavy jars balanced on their heads. We greeted them with a *Buenos dias* and they answered with a "Go with God" that itself was enough to show that we were far from the hustle and noise of cities. Boys and men were driving flocks of brown goats across the red marshes. Now and then the goats would stop to snatch at a fig-cactus' fruit, but the dogs were always at their heels to prevent their separating themselves from the rest.

Then we came to the first white house in the town, where the street begins to slope upwards, and there four other boys attached themselves to us. At the cinema, to which an aged film occasionally comes, we were reinforced by another dozen. When we reached the ruins of the old castle that lie by themselves on the top of a steep hill overlooking the town and the church, I turned and counted our train: there were seventy-eight.

It is not every day that foreigners come to Palos.

Before we left home we had arranged that our letters should be sent to us Poste Restante, c/o Post Office, Palos, and we now wanted to fetch them. It took us twenty minutes to find the post office. People don't write much in Palos. Eventually we discovered it in the main street. There was no sign outside, nothing to distinguish it from the other buildings. It was just a bare wall on to the street, with a dark hole here and there which were the windows, and a black hole leading into the earth which was the door. Down into this I plunged, while Niels and Jens entertained the children. It was an easy job. All they needed to do was to stand still and talk with each other, and at once every single one of the seventy-eight giggled.

I reached a gloomy hall in which sat an old woman plucking a hen, and an old man snoring in a rocking-chair. Outside in the sunlit patio, the centre of the house, bloomed shrilly red bushes of Christmas stars, and down from the roof trailed some creeper with deep lilac flowers. No, they didn't have any letters for the *Santa Maria*. No, not for the *Pinta* or *Niña* either. Nowhere could I see a sign of postal activity, so I asked the old man to make a search. He pulled up his trousers and, getting out of his rocking-chair, walked across to the window. Reaching his hand in behind a flower-pot he pulled out a packet of letters tied together with string. We untied the string and looked through them. There were about twenty letters, but none were marked " Poste Restante " and none were for us, but there was one from England which had been lying there a couple of years already. There was no address on the back to say who had sent it, so I suggested to the postmaster that we should open it and see if by any chance it was urgent. He had once thought of doing that a year before, he said, but then he had forgotten about it.

It was from a sailor asking the authorities to obtain for him the address of a girl he had once known. Her name was Carmen.

We threw it into the waste-paper basket.

Then I asked whether there were any registered letters. Yes, there were. Would we like to have a look at them. We would. He walked off and opened a drawer in the wash-stand. There among hair-brushes and bottles of brilliantine lay the four or five letters. But none were for us.

We had been almost a month late in arriving because of the contrary winds into which we had run, and it was quite unthinkable that no one had written to us. There must be some letters for one or other of us. I explained this to the postmaster, but he was now anxious to return to his rocking-chair and was coming to regard me as a rather tiresome customer. If any of you have ever arrived in a foreign port expecting letters from home, you will understand our feelings as we set off back down the street.

Outside the town hall which was no more different from the other buildings than the post office, we met a man in a blue shirt and a week-old stubble. Were we from the *Santa Maria*, he asked? Were we expecting any letters? We were. He handed us a bundle.

A few days later, when we were in Rabida, another man came up to us. He had nothing to do with the post office, but he gave us three or four letters, one of which was registered. I never found out how it was that they had got into his possession without the postmaster knowing anything about them. But at any rate we received about half the letters sent to us. The others were sent back, marked " Return to sender ", because the address was unknown. The significance of the words "poste restante" has evidently not been explained to those responsible in that part of the international postal union which goes by the name of Palos. That we got any letters at all was due to my dear mother who with her own hands had sewn " Santa Maria " in easily legible letters across our sky-blue sweaters before we left. I sent her an extra grateful thought.

The children politely accepted the Danish stamps we offered them, but then just threw them down. Palos is so far off the beaten track that its children do not collect stamps. Nice little Palos that doesn't even possess a hotel; faithful little Palos, that with complete disregard for Christopher Columbus stubbornly maintains that it was its own Martin Pinzon who discovered America, and so renounces all the tourist trade that the much smarter Franciscan brothers of Rabida have attracted just through developing the highly doubtful legend of how poor, misunderstood Columbus arrived tired and thirsty at the monastery gate, and how the abbot was the first man to appreciate his idea, and how this resulted in the queen allowing herself to be overpersuaded, with the result that the Genoese got his chance.

Rabida has monopolized Columbus, while Palos lies forgotten behind its hills beside the red river. The Rabida myth is highly suspect, while Palos' account is historically sound. But Palos stands by Martin Pinzon and so must scratch its money out of the yellow-ochre earth with primitive wooden ploughs beneath a blazing sun. That, perhaps, is why, when anyone from a distant land comes there who remembers the name of Pinzon and is willing to recognize the part the brothers played in the history of discovery, all hearts are opened to him and Anis Pinzon flows in the Bar Pinzon in the shadow of the Pinzon statue; and, if they have come by ship, a pale shy woman in black clothes will come aboard and tell them that Pinzon was one of her ancestors.

CHAPTER VII

The Dancing Class

AN endless expanse baking in the sun, contours that disappear away under the horizon in a mixture of heat and reddish-yellow dust. A hedge of fig-cactus; nearby another of large grey-blue agaves. Chattering girls in a vineyard bending over bulging baskets, and straightening up to offer the stranger a bunch of grapes heavy with juice. A herdsman slowly driving a herd of red-brown pigs across the high ground. Over the crest of the hill gallops a horseman. He halts for a moment and looks about him, one hand shielding his eyes from the glaring sun. Over his head he has draped a handkerchief that hangs down over his shoulders leaving only his face free. On top he wears a beret. Seen silhouetted against the pale haze of the horizon he resembles a nomad of the desert. Far down the dusty road, in the distance, a cart rumbles slowly along behind its span of four mules : gypsies on the move.

That is Andalusia.

Grey-green groves of olives, almond trees, occasional tufts of cotton, a train standing puffing in a little town where there is no shade, white houses that reflect the sunlight and dazzle the man who slowly creeps along by the house walls. There is a dead dog in the gutter. It has lain there several days, for no one can be bothered to remove it. Its skin has become taut as the merciless sun dries it to a mummy. The women raise their heads for an instant as the stranger walks past, then look down again bashfully at the ground and go on with their work.

A man drives his primitive wooden plough into the crumbling dry earth and calls to his supine mule.  Jerking and leaping the plough glides along an inch or two under the stone-hard crust.

The river lies dead between the yellowy-brown mud of the banks. There is no current and the water is as brown as mild ale. The mud is baked and riven with cracks several inches deep. Away in the distance a boat with a pointed lateen sail glides indolently along. The sail is swollen like a balloon, though up here inland there is not a breath of air to be felt, not a hint of the coolness for which we long.

Evening comes and the sun goes down in a colourful splendour that disregards all accepted rules. The countryside now has a purple glow over it; the sky in the west flames with the strongest and warmest colours of the spectrum, but up towards the zenith it is still deep blue. Soon, however, the deep blue turns to dark violet and a host of large bright stars design a pattern of light above the fields, vineyards and villages. Slowly the clouds of dust settle, and towards midnight the horizon is clear. The night is like soft velvet.

A young woman came towards me in the garden and stretched out her cupped hands in which lay piled freshly plucked heads of the true jasmin. The scent of them rose into my face as I bent down and almost stupefied me. The young woman eyes were like

The old church in Palos, where Columbus prayed

Fruits of the South (Niels Underbjerg)

pieces of the night sky, soft bits of black velvet in which sparks had caught.

Cicadas were scraping away on their fiddles in the gardens round about, in the country beyond, and far out into the darkness.

Andalusia.

Awnings stretched over narrow alleys that seem ready to froth over with all the life that is crowded into them in the short hours before the somnolence of noon descends upon Seville. Here in the old streets each house has its balcony, each balcony its lattice-work; each door is a gem of the art of working iron in which imagination has played on the Arabian motives that here and there are hewn into the marble above some gateway dating from the days when the Moors ruled in Spain. Inhospitably the houses turn their backs on the passer-by, white naked backs in which doors and windows are like black holes, yet they open inwards on to sunlit patios where flowers spill down from lips of great red earthenware jars, or creepers hide the pattern of colourful tiles, where birds sing in gilded cages and slender jets of water tinkle down into the basins of fountains.

The bars are hospitably open to the pavement. They have golden wines in carafes and sweet liqueurs. Flat Spanish hats crown deeply chiselled Spanish faces; now and again you will catch a glimpse of a Moorish profile, or an inquisitive glance shot at you over the rim of a gaudy fan that you can see folding and opening with indolent grace above the iron rim of a balcony. Shoe-blacks swarm like flies, and lottery

tickets and American cigarettes are offered for sale a
every street corner.

A poor woman begs for bread and she means *bread*
for the moment you stretch out your hand with the
remains of your luncheon roll she pounces on it like a
wolf and devours it to the last crumb; then she crosses
herself and disappears in the throng. Broad bandoliers
and red tassels of officers hurrying past; black priests
shuffling noiselessly by in clumsy rubber-soled boots;
flies buzzing round over-ripe bunches of grapes in
the old quarter; a hurdy-gurdy playing on the Avenida
along which yellow taxis twine their way through the
crowds, a water-seller crying his precious cooling wares
that he carries in a gigantic earthenware jar hung on
the back of a tired old donkey that no longer has the
energy to whisk the flies away with its tousled old
tail; children with bare bottoms playing in the middle
of the street—Seville.

There is a certain little house in the Rua Espiritu
Santo. Whenever you pass it you will hear coming
from it the sound of someone monotonously hammering on a worn-out piano. It goes on hour after hour.
Sometimes that monotonous jangle is accompanied
by the rhythmic stamp of heels on a stone floor. The
street door stands ajar.

It was shadowy in the room. It was only twelve feet
broad and twenty long. The walls were white-washed
and decorated with pictures of saints, a couple of
bracket lamps and some painted plates. The piano was
as aged as from the sound outside you had guessed
it to be. It had roses carved on the music-rest,
and curly legs. At it sat an old man playing away with

dead cigar between his unshaven lips. Mechanically
e repeated the tune over and over and over again.
long the walls sat old women with dark upper lips,
oung women, girls of ten or so, and a couple of
ouths of eighteen or twenty. The floor was of
one mosaic.

In one corner stood a manikin. The sleeves of his
lue shirt were rolled up, the collar wide open at the
eck round which a gold amulet dangled on a chain.
Ie was half bald and very fat. A belt divided his body
nto two spheres on top of which was a third, his head.
Ie had a pronounced limp. So this was *El Cojo*,
"The Lame One," the famous Dancing Master of
eville.

In front of him were three young men and a girl.
The men were broad shouldered, narrow-hipped,
ithe as eels, like rapiers; the girl as slim as a grey-
hound, soft-hipped. The men were mere youths of
seventeen or eighteen, she twenty. The men had the
slightly weak features of the gypsy with their coarse
dark brown hair, big noses and receding chins.

The piano thumped. El Cojo clicked his fingers
like castanets and it sounded as though they too were
made of hard wood, and so the four danced. She in
front, gliding from one to the other, now at a distance
now enticingly near, now slipping away, now brush-
ing a shoulder—just to glide off again with eyes like
blazing coals. The three young men, who were mere
slender youths, stamped their heels on the floor in a
provocative irresistible rhythm that thundered through
that little room, a bewitching rhythm, breathless and
not to be denied. You forgot the stifling atmosphere

the stench of sweat, the reek of garlic. You no longer
saw the cheap pictures on the walls. You no longer
noticed that the girl was wearing a cheap crumpled
blouse and a stained skirt, that the youths' trousers
were frayed at the bottom, or that two of them wore
braces over their wet cheap shirts, while the third had
tied his round his waist so that his brown skin shone
damply in the space between shirt and trousers.

El Cojo's cracking fingers seemed to be flinging
the provocative rhythm at the four dancers. The girl
answered with explosive snapping castanets. On and
on they danced beneath the low ceiling of that little
room, a dance that was the whole ardent soul of
Andalusia, that burst the walls and filled the universe,
till there was nothing but the sound of castanets, the
stamp of heels and the fiery glint of dark eyes. It was
a dance akin to the obsessing rhythm of the jungle's
drums, sprung from the same root, but refined
throughout the centuries till it could express more
varied emotions than just the blood-lust and terror
of the jungle. There was fervour, erotism, frenzy,
jubilation, defiance and coquetry in it, but no sadness,
no gentle little smiles, no semitones.

It was Andalusia that danced there in that little room
in the Rua Espiritu Santo. The four nameless dancers
on its dirty stone floor could have appeared on any
stage in the world and they would have been acclaimed
as fervently as they danced, however spoilt the
audience. They would have captivated the most
blasé " house ", kindled a flame in the soul of the
most reserved of Englishmen and made him forget
his complexes, for the Andalusian rhythm is as

catching as the plague, and its dance would melt an iceberg.

It is, however, but very rarely that Andalusia's dancers ever go beyond their country's frontiers. The world beyond the Pyrenees is banned territory full of fearful dangers and hostile mysteries, the same sort of world as was depicted on the maps and charts of the days when the first Spanish explorers had to force their crews to sail across unknown oceans; a world of creatures half man, half beast, and of dragons that breathed out fire. In this world across the mountains live beings who do not speak Spanish, who do not even cook with oil; people who permit their daughters to go alone to the cinema with a young man to whom they are merely betrothed. There are countries there in whose churches women sit with uncovered heads, countries where mothers of small children show themselves publicly in bathing dress. And in these countries there are people who like the dances of America; some are even so strange that they are fond of fox-trots and jitterbug.

" Sheer mechanics," said El Cojo. " Brilliant and admirable, but all automatic ; arms and legs like well-oiled pistons. But where is there any soul in it? What fervour or sense is there in those dances?

" When we dance, we are in love. We are unhappy, our joy is unbridled, we are sad, we are playful; but we are never insensible machines just executing a series of intricate steps in a fixed definite order without expressing through them anything that is within ourselves.

"Nor are you ever likely to see a Spanish dancer attempting a Viennese waltz. He would be unable to dance it. Yet there are few foreign dancers who won't sometime try to do a Spanish dance. It is very seldom —and I'm being as kind as I can—that they succeed."

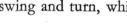

El Cojo sent his four pupils back to their places against the wall and a young girl stepped forward. Her mother sat on a bench watching her, her eyes as sharp and alert as a sea-eagle's.

Spanish girls spend the first quarter of their lives being guarded by dragon-mothers. Then they get married and spend the remaining three-quarters of their lives guarding their daughters like dragons with young. The only exceptions are those who in one way or another go wrong, who fall in love and step off the narrow traditional path. They never return to the family fold. Decent men turn their backs on them. They become dancers or take the downward path that leads them to the decent men, when they have left their wives behind at home.

The little girl stepped out into the middle of the floor and began to dance tentatively, nervously. She put her feet wrong. El Cojo walked in front of her and slid into the dance, showing her the steps. She was lovely, delicate, enchanting; he was middle-aged, fat and bald.

At first, he just looked ridiculous. The sweat was pouring off his bald pate; his shirt was soaking on his back and under his arms. And he was lame. But then he began to move his arms; his feet began to stamp rhythmically, his heavy flabby body to bend and swing and turn, while his fingers acted as castanets. And then suddenly you had forgotten that he was fat and flabby; you no longer even saw the beads of sweat; you were aware of nothing but the graceful, lovely movements as rhythmically and easily he glided about the floor. The prince had found his voice and was talking through the toad's mouth.

El Cojo danced—and stole the picture. You no longer noticed the young girl; but you realized why it was that men and women dancers from all Spain came to the Rua Espiritu Santo and passed through the mouldering wooden doorway into that little room, for there they could find fresh inspiration, learn new patterns for the feet to weave. The pianist picked up a guitar. Castanets clattered . . . Andalusia.

Andalusia, that is Seville, and Palos, and Moguer, and Rabida; the last part of the old world that Columbus saw before he set out on his long expedition into the unknown, and the part of Spain that supplied him with his three caravels and 120 picked seamen.

It was night and the jasmin was pouring out its scent. Oranges hung heavy with juice on the trees. The cicadas were scraping away on their fiddles and the quavering notes of a guitar vibrated out into the warm darkness from some invisible balcony.

Why on earth did Christopher Columbus ever leave Andalusia?

71

CHAPTER VIII

The First Stage

AT last the morning came when slowly, link by link, the anchor-chain slipped through the hawse-hole, while *Santa Maria's* bows swung in the ebbing tide that tugged and gasped as it tried to drag her out to sea. The pawls of the windlass clanked over the rusty cogs, now quicker, now slower, as the brown backs of Niels and Jens alternately bent and straightened over the handle of the crank. The Spanish flag fluttered in the morning breeze from one horn of the cross-trees, the Stars and Stripes from the other. The Blue Peter was hoisted at the masthead and the Dannebrog waved gaily from the mizzen top.

At last we were to set sail. Down in the saloon sat the alcalde of Palos, my faithful friend of the last eight eventful days. We now called each other by our christian names. He had invited me to a farewell dinner in his house the evening before and had informed me that now and for ever and ever his house was also my house; he had now come aboard to visit me and I had a feeling that I was expected to recipro-cate and assure him that my ship should also be his ship for ever and ever, and what's more, not only his but his wife's and his four children's and their nurse's and his mother-in-law's as well, for they had all come aboard with him. They had arrived at seven o'clock

72

Leaving the mouth of the Rio Tinto—the voyage proper begins

Niels and Jens do some cleaning

and, although I had told him that we were going to start at eight o'clock as Columbus had done, the alcalde had dismissed their boat and told the man that he would not be required for some time. After that, they had gone straight down to the cabin and had set about unpacking a huge picnic basket. They presented us with a large bottle of wine and several mighty bunches of grapes, and then sat back and waited for us to produce some more of the fine cheese, strong beer and luscious ham with which I had entertained him on previous occasions when he had come aboard alone. And of course we had to offer them our Italian Vermouth and our Danish brandy, to say nothing of our plump Dutch cigars.

The alcalde sat there and enumerated them all, letting his wife and mother-in-law and his four children and their nurse know just how good they had been and so forcing me to set them on the table one by one. He forgot nothing. Not even the butter. His mother-in-law was very fond of butter, and the moment she had sunk her long fangs into a piece of our bread and butter and cheese, she demanded a two pound tin to take ashore with her. I had not met the mother-in-law before and so I refused, saying that we only had that one tin. That made her furious and she refused to say another word to me all the time they were aboard, and it was a long time.

The cheese disappeared as though it had been a snowball on a kitchen range. The ham vanished in the twinkling of an eye, and so did the beer and the vermouth and the brandy. When there was nothing, not a crumb, left, the children began on the grapes they had brought and by the time they were finished there was not a ripe one left. However, we were allowed to keep the wine.

I was on my feet, the perfect smiling host, the whole time. Then the alcalde and one of his children developed stomach-ache. That wouldn't have mattered so much if they had understood the pump system of our lavatory, but they didn't. Another of the children found that the ham disagreed with it, and collapsed.

It was now a quarter to eight, and Columbus had started at eight o'clock exactly. The alcalde stuck his head out of the lavatory door to tell me how little importance he attached to that. I have seldom met a nicer or more helpful person than Antonio, but I hate to be late. So, at ten minutes to eight I told Jens to start the engine. The mother-in-law pricked her ears and began packing away the last remaining pieces of ham in her basket. At five minutes to eight the anchor hung clear at the bows. At eight o'clock exactly *Santa Maria* began slowly to swing round. A couple of the children ran up on deck to see what was happening and, when they did, they seemed to find it highly diverting. Meanwhile the alcalde sat in the lavatory with our visitors' book on his knees busy writing an official farewell message from the town of Palos. He had even brought his official stamp with him.

Fifteen minutes later we lay off Rabida monastery. There were a few early-risers standing on the jetty and they waved to us. The bells in the slender tower were ringing for mass just as they had done the day Columbus slipped slowly past downstream on the ebbing tide. To myself I cursed my dear friend the alcalde, because he and his wife and his mother-in-law, his four children and their nurse were ruining the whole atmosphere. Then the alcalde's head appeared above the hatchway.

"Where are we?" he asked.

"Rabida," said I. "Next stop the Bahamas," I went on, trusting that he didn't remember that Columbus had gone ashore in between on the Canary Islands, only six days out from Spain.

"God save us," ejaculated the alcalde, good catholic that he was, and his head disappeared as he dashed for the saloon and swept his children together and up on deck. His wife and mother-in-law followed with expressions of injured innocence and the remains of our hospitality in paper parcels under their arms. The nurse giggled.

I had waved to the people on shore to send out a boat, and the moment it arrived we stuffed the alcalde and all his belongings into it, cast off their rope and let them drive. After that we were able to smile naturally and we lined up in the stern, dipped our flag in honour of Antonio and the monastery, and gave three cheers for Palos. Antonio, however, paid no attention. He was urging the boatmen most insistently, for he had to get ashore—quickly.

Such was the departure of *Santa Maria* from the little lost and forgotten town of Palos in Andalusia. She was now outward bound for the New World and great adventure. The clang of the monastery's bells

died away. There on the coast ahead was a little
round grey tower. The Romans had built it many
centuries ago as part of the defences of the entrance
to the two rivers. It had already stood there for many
hundreds of years that morning Columbus put to sea.
We greeted it with due deference, wishing that the
generations since Columbus had done as much, for
then they would not have put a wooden tank on top
of it and turned it into a cistern to provide water for
the cannery inland. *Ave Caesar*!

Then the tower had slipped astern, and we had to
keep a look-out for the buoys marking the channel
that would take us across the sand bar in the falling
tide. We met a Dutch boat, the *Niejmegen* from the
Hague, and trawler after trawler going home after the
exertions of the night heavily burdened with sardines.
And so we crossed the bar and turned as close in
ashore as we dared, for we had promised the lighthouse keeper that we would. He was standing on the
top balcony where he had assembled his whole family
and seemingly most of his friends, and as we drew
abreast he slowly hauled down the flag. We dipped
ours three times, the greatest sign of respect a ship
can show, and then we altered course and stood away
to the south-west. Gradually the coast of Andalusia
faded until it was no more than a reddish golden strip.

In the vicinity of the river estuary there were
scattered patches of brown and green, but a few miles
to the south all vegetation ceases and there the golden
desert of stone comes down to the very shore, parched
and merciless, stretching away to the south as far as
the eye can reach without as much as a building, a

lighthouse, or a sea-mark to protrude and break its flatness. That, too, is how it must have looked on that other 3rd August all those many years ago. Our last impression of Europe must have been the same for Columbus and for us.

Then we lost sight of land and darkness fell. All the stars came out above our heads and we were able to put out the binnacle-light and steer by their constellations. There is nothing more lovely than to be able on a tropically warm night to stand on the deck of a sailing ship from which comes the smell of tar and feel the breeze cool your cheeks, while you keep the jib-boom pointing right at the spot where the Milky Way and the sea meet on the horizon. Astern, the water makes its own milky way of sparkling phosphorescence that stretches on and on and on until it too meets the sky. The water gurgles and laughs as it slips rustling past the ship's sides, and the hours fly so fast that the watch is over before you realize it. Yet the night is so warm that you go to the bows and stand there long after you are free to go below and sleep, stand and gaze out across the ocean and down at the myriads of glittering particles in the bow waves with not a thought in your head, just relaxing, revelling in the freedom and beauty of it all.

Away behind on land the telegraph wires are probably humming, loudspeakers wailing: fresh sensational news, new friction between the great powers, new stumbling blocks in the path of peace. But it was not for us to turn on that drivelling depressing machine.

Suddenly the sun got up. The wind dropped and we began to roll in a long big swell. In the commotion of our farewells and the fine weather of the last few hours we had completely forgotten to clear the ship. The deck was littered with everything conceivable, and down in the cabin the empty glasses and bottles still stood where the alcalde and his family had left them. A cupboard door in the pantry flew open and seven saucers shot out along with the skipper's fine new cup that he had bought the day before in Palos. Then the squall swept down upon us. The rigging shrieked and *Santa Maria* heeled right over on her side. Two cases with empty bottles collided and careered together across the deck and back again until every bottle in them was broken and half the pieces lay scattered about the deck. Jens was at the wheel and unable to leave it, for most of the time we were driving along with the the end of the main boom under water, and so it was I who had to clamber up the companion-way and out into the thundering darkness on deck in an attempt to pick up some of the broken glass and throw it overboard. I shall never do that again in pyjamas and bare feet.

During the next watch Niels had all the Gibraltar traffic, great liners blazing with lights one after the other; but then they moved farther and farther to the north, and in the end we were alone. There wasn't a wisp of smoke anywhere on the horizon, not a flying fish, not a dolphin. The sea was dead.

There was nothing to enter in the log under the heading "work and incidents". Nor, judging from his log, was Columbus' sail across this stretch of sea any more eventful.

Friday, August 3rd, 1492. Set sail from the bar of Saltes at 8 o'clock, and proceeded with a strong breeze till sunset, sixty miles or fifteen leagues S. Afterwards S.W. and S. by W. which is the direction of the Canaries. Saturday, August 4th. Steered S.W. by S. Sunday, August 5th. Sailed day and night more than forty leagues.

The wind had died down again and *Santa Maria* was running placidly over a sea that was incredibly blue. There was time now to write up the log, to wash our clothes and kill off the flies, hundreds of which had come aboard while we were on the river, vicious pale grey Spanish flies that bite each time they settle. We had reached the end of our potatoes and now sampled the sack of dried ones we had in reserve. We put them to soak for six hours, then for twenty-four hours; we tried to boil them, then to fry them, then to boil them first and fry them afterwards, but nothing we could do would make them edible.

Columbus had other worries on his voyage from Palos to the Canaries. The Canaries had been transferred to Spain under a treaty signed with Portugal in 1480. For Columbus they were a convenient springboard, a last station at which he could replenish his provisions and supplies of water, but he was to find other uses for them. On the voyage down the *Pinta's* rudder developed a fault. They repaired it as well as they could in the open sea, but then it went wrong again and they had to put in to the island of Gran Canarie and repair the damage properly. Martin Alonzo Pinzon was in command of the *Pinta* and he stayed with her while Columbus sailed on to Gomera, supposedly to try and find another ship to take the place of the seemingly somewhat frail *Pinta*. He also took advantage of the enforced wait to have the smallest of his ships, the *Niña* rerigged. The *Niña* was commanded by Martin's brother, Vincente Yanez Pinzon. She had left Palos with the lateen rig beloved of the Mediterranean, but that elegant pointed sail had proved unsuitable for sailing the Atlantic, and so she was to have a square sail such as the other two caravels had.

While these repairs were being carried out in what to-day is the large harbour of Las Palmas, Columbus was making good use of his time on Gomera, where the people helped him forage. He made the acquaintance of the islanders' ruler, the young and beautiful Doña Beatriz, widow of the late governor. A deal has been hinted about these two, but the official biographies of Columbus pay no attention to such rumours. However, we are getting too far ahead. Let us go back to his journal.

Wednesday, August 8th. There were divers opinions among the pilots of the three vessels, as to their true situation, and it was found that the admiral was the most correct.

There was no such disagreement among us. To be candid, on that fourth day none of us had the least idea where we were, and admitted it. In the first place, the engine had started missing and had had to be stopped, so that we could track down the fault. Then, the sun had failed to show itself at the times it is supposed to appear so that you can take an observation; but, even if it had come out, our half-chronometer was not in a position to tell us the exact time for it had gained 2 minutes 41 seconds on the first day out, 1 minute 52 seconds on the second, and 3 minutes 5 seconds on the third. It had never been quite normal since the clockmaker in Guernsey had put a new spring in it. The only thing we were sure of was that we had been carried a considerable distance by the current. We were thus curious to see whether the first land to appear on tne misty horizon would be Africa, the Canaries, or something really surprising. In Neils' view we had already passed the Canaries, so our next landfall would in all probability be the ice-barrier by the South Pole. However, he had always had an itch to go whaling, so that was obviously just wishful thinking.

In the evening of our fifth day out we sighted land ahead. It was the northern point of Teneriffe. When Columbus sighted the peak of Teneriffe "which is a lofty mountain," they saw "a great eruption of flames" coming from it. The Pico de Teide, over 13,000 feet high, has grown more peaceable with the years and we saw no flames. To-day it emits a little sulphureous vapor from the small holes round the crater whose foot is nearly always hidden in cloud, and that is all. When we sighted it, it was a dark silhouette away in the depths of the night. All trace of man's presence and activities had disappeared in the darkness. It looked grim and unapproachable. So, too, it must have appeared in Columbus' day when watchful straining Guancho eyes followed the progress of his caravels from the shore, anxiously wondering whether this were another Spanish attempt on the large island which despite their superior weapons the Spaniards had not yet been able to

conquer. However, Columbus and his little fleet sailed past and so did we.

The next morning we ran into the little bay on the north-eastern coast of Gomera in which Columbus had also sought refuge. Among the feathery tops of the date-palms on shore we could see a square tower, all that remained of the castle in which the lovely Doña Beatriz had lived. Across the red roofs of the houses we glimpsed the little red steeple of the church in which Columbus had said his last devotions before continuing his voyage.

We lowered the " Caramel " into the water and rowed ashore. The " Caramel " was our little dinghy.

CHAPTER IX

The Isle of Gomera

CHRISTOPHER COLUMBUS never went to Teneriffe. Gomera was his island. He visited it on each of his voyages except the fourth and last. He said that he would not go to Terneriffe because the island was in the hands of the savage Guanchoes, which is a pretty poor excuse coming from a man who had just set out to cross uncharted seas with the object of discovering and subjecting new lands whose inhabitants, according to the accounts of trustworthy seafarers, were great warriors, had dogs' heads and lizards' tails, breathed out fire from their mouths, and lived on a cannibal's diet. However, I suppose Columbus had to have some excuse for his visits to Gomera that he could tell his wife when he wrote home, but the historians and we know better.

It was on Gomera that the young and beautiful Doña Beatriz lived. The historians have been very discreet. They do mention his visit to that merry widow, but quickly add that he only stayed there while *Pinta* was repairing her rudder at Gran Canarie, and that that took three weeks. Three weeks to repair a rudder on a ship that had a crew of thirty or forty men! That is hardly convincing. And why didn't Columbus stay at Gran Canarie and see that the work was pushed ahead? What sort of an admiral is it who leaves one of his ships just at the moment when he

ought to be frantically eager to get away and continue the voyage as quickly as possible? No, at this juncture, in my opinion, he didn't care tuppence about *Pinta*, *Niña*, or *Santa Maria*, because he was lying on his back on a divan in the Governor's castle on Gomera letting Doña Beatriz pop large juicy grapes into his mouth one after the other. And I know what the grapes of Gomera are like, for I have tasted them myself. Then, one day at breakfast Doña Beatriz told him that there had been another letter from Queen Isabella in the post asking about him and suggested that it really was time he did a little work for his keep and his country. So, Columbus said "all right," and Doña Beatriz went out on to the balcony and signalled to her people to start getting the provisions and Columbus' sea-chest on board. At which point Columbus' discreet scribe picked up his quill again and made this further entry on his roll of parchment:

" *Having taken in wood, water, meat and other provisions . . . the admiral took his final departure from Gomera with the three vessels. . . .* "

There seems to be a world of relief behind that little word "final."

Gomera has not forgotten Columbus, nor the lovely Beatriz whom the history books pass over so lightly. The island's member in the Spanish parliament, Pascasio Trujille, was in Madrid agitating for the construction of a gigantic lighthouse that would serve as a visible reminder of the fact that Gomera was the actual jumping-off place for three of Columbus' voyages across the Atlantic. The islanders themselves point proudly to the old square watch-tower which once was part of the lovely Beatriz' castle, and every year at the beginning of October when the grapes hang heavy from the knotty branches of the vines, and the huge bunches of bananas begin to ripen, and the hillsides grow red with tomatoes, Gomera celebrates its greatest festival of the year. There is of course, a highly colourful procession and in it walks the year's Doña Beatriz dressed in a reckless frock of white tulle and accompanied by a suite of pages and ladies-in-waiting. She is chosen from among the loveliest maidens in the little town of San Sebastian, and you must realize that both women and grapes grow sweet and lovely under the sun of Gomera.

We lowered the " Caramel " into the water and rowed ashore. When we saw that on the diminutive jetty which comprises the harbour of San Sebastian stood the island's governor, the naval commander, the mayor, his and the governor's secretary, and the senior customs officer, waiting to give us an official welcome, we were very glad that the previous day we had given the " Caramel " a new coat of shiny white paint and that before going ashore we had changed from shorts and bare chests, our normal dress, into our ceremonial tropical uniforms. For the first time since September 1492 a *Santa Maria* had dropped anchor off Doña Beatriz' town, and the town had prepared us a reception that I shall never forget. Did I say " the town"? I meant the island.

With the governor on my left, the naval commander on my right, and the rest of the company three steps behind, I walked up along the main street and across the plaza with its large juicy-green bay-trees to the

government building.   After a short reception there
we continued on to the offices of the naval command
and from there went to the town's sports arena
where several hundred people had gathered expect
antly.   Inside the ring of the spectators stood a
score of powerful young men in two groups.   The
seats consisted partly of backless benches, and partly
of stone terraces, but in one place there was a row
of armchairs. They were for us. As we took our places
a brass band sounded a fanfare. And so the display began

I have never seen Icelandic *glima*, except in photographs, but judging by them I should say that it and
the wrestling of the Canary Islanders, their national
sport, are related.   The wrestlers wear a kind of
sailor's blouse and long blue dungaree trousers with
the legs rolled up to the middle of their thighs, which
they ring like a couple of firm round sausagey cushions.
They take up position facing each other, then they
bend forward at right angles so that their cheeks
touch and take firm hold of each other by the roll of
trouser-leg round their opponent's thighs.   And so
they begin to wrestle.

They heave and pull and twist at those wretched
trousers, wriggle like eels, or stand still waiting for
their opponent's next move, watching each other the
while.   The bout is finished when one of the two is
thrown.   The moment he touches the ground with as
as much as a finger, he is out.   There is none of that
slow torture of having your shoulders pressed down
on the mattress.

The display we watched was given by two champion
teams from the large island of Teneriffe. Although in

its own way quite an exciting form of sport, I found it rather difficult to keep interested in the display for very long. I am not accustomed to sitting in the armchair of honour and did not feel at ease; also the naval commander on my left, nice man though he was, was not what you would call an interesting person and I would gladly have swopped him for a Doña Beatriz. However, though that may be what you are thinking, it is not a thing you can very well say.

Why is that the news-reel reporters are never there when something really important is happening? And why weren't they there the next morning either, when the governor drove down to the jetty to fetch me and I found him sitting there waiting in his big Buick, the largest and most magnificent of the eighteen motor-cars registered on Gomera? As it was, the only reporter to witness my triumphal tour across the mountains and through the fertile valleys of Gomera, was myself; and modesty prevents my describing the events of that tour as lyrically and dramatically as I would have done had I been describing the homage paid to some other great man. And homage is the only word that describes it, homage to the *Santa Maria*.

It was all very well prepared. The telephones must have been ringing all morning up and down the island with the news that Columbus had returned. Once again Columbus was to start a voyage from Gomera, and the people of Gomera were to give him a fitting send-off.

How can I describe Gomera when all superlatives are worn and meaningless, when every fitting phrase is a hackneyed cliché? If only I could borrow the pen of Robert Louis Stevenson, then I could describe this little island that lies off the beaten track and has not even a tourist organization to take it under its wing and ruin its little townships that do not boast even a single hotel where a tourist could eat or stay. Otherwise, I am afraid that what I may say will be no nearer conveying the true spirit and beauty of Gomera than does the coloured picture post card which you send home from the holiday resort where you are staying, even though you have marked the window of your room with a cross.

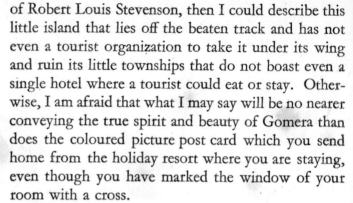

The car wound its way up the steep road with many twists and turns. Deep below us lay the green valley through which runs the little stream on which the existence of the town of San Sebastian depends. The houses were like small white dots, clustered thickly near the blue bay where *Santa Maria* lay rocking at her anchor-chain, and sprinkled more and more thinly up the valley. At intervals along the river bank was a placid ox walking sedately round and round beside a boy of four or five. It was harnessed to a primitive mill that pumped water from the stream to the irrigation channels without which the soil on the weather-beaten hillsides cannot be made to grow the tomatoes, grapes, maize and bananas that are the main crops of Gomera.

With the years, the small industrious men of Gomera have extended their activities further and further up the valley and higher and higher up the hillsides. They have built narrow terraces fenced with stone on slopes so steep that a donkey can scarcely climb them, terraces that are their stepping stones to prosperity.

And so we reached the flat little island of San Salvador with its dangerous rocks,

and, like Columbus, were welcomed by the natives

With the industry of ants they are building on and on, higher and higher. We passed them as we drove along, patient peasants trudging along behind small grey donkeys, without a smile or a nod of greeting for us. On their heads they carried baskets of stones that were to raise the wall of some terrace yet a little higher. Had we stopped them and asked who was Truman or Molotov, they would have shaken their heads without understanding. It is the Middle Ages you meet on these island roads, for these men are bound to their land as effectively as any serf of those olden days. Their horizon stretches no farther than their own fields, and all that they ask of life is their daily bread and a handful of *gofio*. Should you commiserate with them on having to wrest so meagre a subsistence from the hard rock, they would just look at you uncomprehendingly, for they have no means of comparing their lot with that of the little men in other countries. Nor have they any eyes for the savage beauty amongst which they live their sad, industrious lives.

They scarcely heeded the governor and his guests gliding quietly past in a large limousine that for them was like a falling star in the night sky, a greeting from another world with which they never had had, and never would have, any contact. Their destiny lay in the valley whose sides were the enfolding hands of the paternal mountains. On the peaks of these mountains the clouds were tearing themselves to tatters that caught and hung there, shedding mist and drizzle over the upper slopes. Yet, down in the valley the sun was shining.

These mountains rise up steeply from the blue sea to a height of 6,000 feet and more. At 3,000 feet man gives up, at any rate for the present, and all above that remains untouched, as bare and sterile as it was in the days when the Guanchoes fought, retreating from ledge to ledge before the superior weapons of the Spaniards. The conquest of these islands proved excellent training in colonial warfare, so that later, on the other side of the Atlantic, the Spaniards were already experts, experts in the ruthless slaughter of humans. All the same, they had a hard job here on Gomera and it was some time before the island was sufficiently " pacified " for a lovely Beatriz to be able to welcome a Columbus in her lonely castle.

We rounded a crest and slid down into the valley on the north side of the island. Looking away from the reddish-mauve peaks and down into the valley our eyes met a world that was of the purest green : the banana plantations. The whole of this narrow glen and far up the mountainside was covered with neat rows of large banana plants. At the lower end of the great clusters there was already the splendour of the globular mauve banana blossom; the banana harvest was about to begin.

The solid green bunches were carefully tied up and away from the stem so that no gust of wind should be able to bump them against the trunk, for the least little knock causes a black spot to appear and beneath this the banana will rot. Men and women were going from plant to plant selecting bunches and carefully cutting them. Having severed a bunch they would place it on their heads cushioned by a folded sack and so carry it to the packing shed, where each bunch was separately packed in straw, banana leaves and brown paper. Thus swaddled they are sent down to the sea where small steamers and schooners lie waiting beyond the surf to receive them from the crane on the cliffs, whose long arm swings out to them over the sea. When they have a full cargo these little ships take them to Santa Cruz and Las Palmas, where modern fruit boats with air-conditioning and re-frigerators take them at full speed to any country that has the foreign exchange with which to pay for them.

The price of bananas may rise or fall, but the men and women who harvest and pack the green bunches will remain as ragged as they have always been and will continue to gather round a pot that contains nothing but the eternal dreary gofio, a food that may fill their stomachs, but it does not meet their need of food values.

And so we drove down into the little town of Hermigua, and stopped in front of its one and only restaurant. Black-haired men with stubbly beards looked up in amazement from their *cafe con leche* and dominoes. The mayor came hustling out from the town hall with a growing crowd of the curious behind him. He must have had a following of at least fifty by the time he reached the car. He greeted the governor, bowed to me, then pulled two bottles from his pockets. These were bottles of the local wine specially labelled " From the town of Hermigua to *Santa Maria* ". He handed them to me and made a little speech wishing us luck and success in our voyage and assuring us that the thoughts of all in Hermigua

would go with us and that they were glad to have been able to help equip us, though no more than symbolically, as the men of Gomera had our great predecessor centuries before.

I took the bottles, thanked him and shook hands; then I nodded my thanks to the crowd, half wishing to laugh at the picture of myself as centre of attraction, half serious because it *was* strangely moving to remember that these people, who were staring at me out of glassy eyes, were mostly direct descendants of the men and women who had sent barrels of wine, cases of fruit and hogsheads of fresh spring water from the wild mountains, to the crews of the three caravels in the early days of September, 1492.

The governor waved his hand and we drove on across the crests of more mountains and down into more green valleys. Agudo, Vallehermoso, and so on, one little township after the other, each hidden in its green glen and at the entrance to each stood a mayor and a gathering of dark-eyed brown-skinned men, women and children, waiting to present me with a gift of the township's special produce. Two bottles of brandy here, two bottles of sweet fragrant palm-honey there, a mighty bunch of bananas, the finest in the valley, a box of sweet yellow dates, an armful of heavy violet bunches of grapes, and so the car became gradually filled as we drove along.

When we returned to the island's capital, the pleasant little town of San Sebastian, the governor's wife was waiting with a dinner she herself had composed in our honour. *There* was the governor, *there* the alcalde, *there* the priest from the church in which

Columbus had worshipped before he set out, praying especially to St. Carmen, the patron saint of the seafarer. Gomera welcomed us and thanked us for coming, wished us luck on our voyage in the wake of the three caravels, and drank to our success in fragrant Sauterne and sweet Malaga.

Through the window I could see the silhouette of Doña Beatriz' castle tower, behind which the sun was setting in a mighty blaze, and the figure of a peasant bowed over his primitive wooden plough. He called encouragingly to his heavy oxen : one last furrow to end the day. Outside in the patio the canaries were preparing for sleep in their gilt cages, sticking their heads under their wings. There was a dead calm in the bay, and *Santa Maria* lay there, like some graceful seabird with folded wings mirroring itself in the glassy water that gradually assumed the red and golden colours of the sunset. Someone was playing a guitar in the street outside. The smoke from the priest's Havana cigar wound up towards the richly carved ceiling.

We were not Catholics—the priest had asked us that—but this was the last evening before we set sail, and so, when we had finished our coffee and liqueurs and got up from the table, I suggested that we should all go to the age-old church. The priest excused himself, but the rest of us went.

The sun had just disappeared behind the mountains and the whole world seemed to be at rest in ineffable peace and slowly fading iridescence. It was the time of day when the stars come out one after the other and settle themselves for their nocturnal watch, and when the land breeze sends a waft of flower-scented coolness through the valley. But in the plaza people were sitting under the bay trees in the sharp glare of electric light bulbs hidden in their crests. They sat at small tables discussing the day's happenings and the latest folly of the big world, but soon they would get up and go each to his home.

The age-old carved door of the church creaked on its rusty hinges and we walked into the dusky interior. Here and there in a corner or angle a lone candle glowed before some saint's altar. A patch of deeper black was the vague shape of a woman absorbed in silent prayer on a prie-dieu. Gold gleamed dully from an altar-piece here, an ornament there, and the light of the candles woke warm answering glints in the dusty lustres under the roof.

What an old, old church it was.

Carefully I placed a candle in a holder in front of St. Carmen's picture and stood there for a while, watching the orange flame glowing under its slender spiral of smoke; then I dipped my finger in a holy-water basin, touched my forehead and chest, turned and walked out. When I emerged back into the warm darkness outside, I had no feeling of having thrust my way in where I had had no business to be. Merciful Carmen, I thought, pray also for us; for tomorrow we set sail along Columbus' route westwards across the sea.

CHAPTER X

Don Juan leads us astray

EARLY the next morning we began preparing to weigh anchor. The sky was empty of clouds and the Trades were blowing steadily out in the bay. As we were busy hauling the dinghy aboard, the skipper saw our friend the Governor come hurrying down to the bridge and behind him a dozen men dragging a heavy wooden case. Behind them again staggered a youth under a heavy sack. Those two things, the sack and the case, were to upset all our plans.

We rowed ashore to see what it was the Governor wanted, leaving Niels in the cabin making our morning coffee. The Governor welcomed us with a beaming smile and told us that he had kept his parting gift to us until this moment for he wanted to give us something that was alive, that would give us great joy and be of great importance to us on our long voyage across the seas.

Something alive? What did he mean? The wildest ideas suggested themselves. For a moment I even thought that perhaps the town of San Sebastian, Gomera's capital, might be going to extremes and giving us a Doña Beatriz to take with us on the voyage. Our knees quaked as we walked towards the large wooden case.

We peered inside. It was no dark-haired Doña Beatriz we saw, but a black-haired pig grunting and frisky after a good night's rest, but with a malevolent gleam in its eyes.

"Fresh food for you," said the Governor. "Something to eat on the voyage, when you are tired of things out of tins."

Jens and the skipper bent down so as to hide the expression on their faces, and tickled the black pig behind the ears, while I voiced our gratitude for so handsome a gift in words that even I felt were excessive considering what we were all thinking.

"Never," said I, "would we forget Gomera." That was true. "Such generosity moved us deeply." That too, in a way was true. "Gomera and Denmark would always be friends, and . . . ." Where in heaven's name were we going to put the brute?

In my mind's eye I could see the deck already so cluttered with spars and cases of Carlsberg, formalin, herrings, and salt meat, coils of rope, blocks, buckets, tanks and drums of oil, that it was hardly possible to find anywhere to put our feet when we had to take in sail in the darkness of night. And now here was another wooden crate a good six feet by four! Where on earth were we going to put it?

However, there was no refusing such a gift, and so the great packing case and its pig and the thirty kilos of maize that went with it were man-handled into the Caramel.

"Remember, two kilos of maize a day," shouted the Governor as we rowed away. "And, of course, all the kitchen scraps."

As we laid alongside *Santa Maria*, Niels emerged out of the cabin, puce in the face from struggling

The first landscape Columbus saw in the New World

Yet, the school-children sang a hymn in its praise

with a refractory primus and in the right frame of mind to expostulate with us for being so long and keeping the coffee waiting.

" What on earth kept you so long? " he began, but then he caught sight of the pig and further words froze at his lips.

"We have brought you a dear little pig," said we.

"It has to have two kilos of maize a day and all the scraps from the galley."

" Who is to look after it? " asked Niels, and there was murder in his eye.

" You! " said we.

" And who will kill it? " he enquired again, running his thumb along the edge of the bread knife he was holding in his hand, but looking at us and not at the pig.

" You! " we said again.

Niels looked from the one of us to the other, just to make sure that we were really in earnest, and, seeing that we were, he grimly demanded to be set ashore.

As he explained, his contract was as seaman and ship's cook, and there was nothing in it about his being pigman and butcher as well. Were he to say " Yes " to the pig, he felt that when we left our next port of call he would probably find himself saddled with a couple of dozen hens running about the fore-deck, to say nothing of the cow tethered in the stern that he would have to milk morning and evening in the intervals between giving turnips and hay to the rabbits which we would have installed in the cable-locker. There was nothing in the Merchant Shipping Act to say that he was to spend six or eight weeks

D 97

looking after a black heathen piglet from Gomera.
And presumably we realized that what we put into
one end of the pig would come out at the other, and
—who was to attend to that?

"You!" we chorused, and heaved the packing
case up on to the rail.

After christening the pig Don Juan de Gomera,
we weighed anchor and sailed away. Meanwhile,
Niels stood glowering at Don Juan, who glared back
at him without even winking. Then we held a short
council of war. It was agreed that we preferred to
keep Niels rather than the pig. This being so, we had
no alternative but to sail the ten hours up to Santa
Cruz on Teneriffe, where I had an old friend in the
Danish Consul. He was an enterprising resourceful
person, who would assuredly be able to relieve us of
Don Juan in such a way that no hint of how cavalierly
we had treated their parting gift should reach the ears
of the Governor and men of Gomera.

Ten hours to Santa Cruz! You can have a lot of
fun with a pair of compasses and a sea-chart, but
sometimes the elements have a nasty habit of making
a fool of theory. We were no sooner clear of the bay
at Gomera than the north-east Trades increased to
storm strength, and, as we were trying to go up along
the east side of Teneriffe, this meant that we got it
right astern. Not only that, but here under the coast
the wind was whipping up seas so choppy and severe
that *Maria* gave in and shook like a jelly each time a
wave came toppling upon her, and as it fell, she would
rear up and fall back again with a smack like a cannon-
shot.

the open fires, and above each entrance there is a streak of black extending up the face of the cliff to show where the smoke has gone.

Inquisitive faces peered shyly at us round all the doors and window openings. Young children stole in and out like frightened mice. The mayor nodded and smiled to every side as we walked along to his father's house, which lay at the farther end, so near to the edge of the cliff that the breakers thundering on the beach below sent the spray spurting up to its paneless windows. Not a bush, not a flower, not a tree.

The old father was head of the clan, a giant of seventy, an old sea-dog, as straight-backed as a grandee, and father of a swarm of children of whom the mayor was the eldest and a rickety boy of thirteen months the youngest. Theirs was the aristocratic family of Abona. They owned the best of the village's dozen fishing boats and also the only motor-vessel that it boasted, the good ship *Amelia* which maintained communications between Santa Cruz and Abona, going back and forwards twice a week with the old man at the wheel, the mayor as deckhand, and a younger brother down in the engine-room. This younger brother was enchanted to hear that we had a Bolinder diesel engine. The *Amelia* also had one. Jens and he thus had an inexhaustible topic of conversation and they chattered away, Jens in Danish, young Gonzales in Spanish, but somehow they seemed to understand each other.

We others drank coffee with Spanish brandy : first with the old man, then with the mayor, then with the young engineer of the *Amelia*, and finally with a married daughter. After that we felt that the time had come when common decency demanded that we should return some of all this hospitality.

The whole family came aboard. It took four trips in our rubber boat to ferry them all across. The old father went on the first trip. He stepped jauntily on to the side of the boat and promptly disappeared under water. However, he crawled smiling aboard again with all the agility of a young man. He looked very funny in the skipper's clothes, for the skipper was a small man whose waist measurement was half that of Gonzales and his legs but two-thirds the length of the Spaniard's.

One of the daughters-in-law sat beside me as we drank our beer and kept telling me that she wasn't an islander, but, thank God, had been born in Madrid. You know the type. Luckily she became seasick after the third glass and had to take her place at the rail beside two other young ladies, and there she stayed for the remainder of their visit.

The rest of us enjoyed ourselves and became friends for life. The engineer helped Jens to clean the filter. The mayor said that the wind would drop in the morning at five o'clock, and his father insisted that he would accompany us to Santa Cruz in the *Amelia*, so as to be on hand in case our motor should again prove fractious. The one Bolinder was to help the other. Eventually we put them ashore with a tin of wheaten flour and a couple of cartons of cigarettes under their arms.

The next morning at five o'clock, when sea and wind had dropped as ordered by the mayor, we put out in the thundering dark through the rocks, and headed north again—to the great regret of Don Juan who could not abide *Maria's* frisky leaps over the long swell. *Amelia* followed us faithfully a short way behind and closer inshore, so as to be ready to get between us and the cliffs should the engine fail us again; but all went well, and before midday Santa Cruz was in sight.

CHAPTER XI

We lose both a pig and a cat

SANTA CRUZ' fashionable yacht club, the Club Nautico, has a swimming pool where various well-born señoritas in diminutive bathing dresses sun their brown limbs. Now it is strictly forbidden in Santa Cruz to sun-bathe in a bathing dress without a skirt, and so the club has erected a ship's bell on which the alarm is sounded whenever a priest or policeman approaches the premises. When it rings the señoritas either dive into the swimming pool or hurriedly fling bathing robes round their charms.

It is the Jesuits who object to sun-bathing. They have a lot to say about things in Santa Cruz. At any rate they have made the Club Nautico incur the expense of buying a bronze bell.

While we were there we discovered that although they have had 450 years in which to do so, the Spaniards have not yet succeeded in pacifying the warlike natives whom Columbus rightly feared. As long as the sun pours down over the town's red roofs and the picturesque streets are crowded, all is lovely and peaceful. The canaries trill gaily in the leafy trees and there isn't a hint of anything being wrong. But when the last gleam of day has vanished behind the top of Pico de Teide, when the little curly Teneriffe poodles are curled up in their baskets and the orchestra is tuning up in the Casino Club, the last of the invincible Guanchoes emerge from the holes in the rocks where they spend the hours of daylight. They creep along the walls of the houses and sneak down the wharfs to the harbour, where they wage partisan war with the whites, as implacable as they were in Columbus' day.

There are no Guanchoes on Gomera. They have all long since been driven out of Abona, but the remaining few who hide in Santa Cruz are very much alive and most effective. Sabotage is their weapon.

Santa Cruz has a nice little harbour. As in all other harbours, it is strictly forbidden to drop any rubbish or refuse into it, yet every night the Guanchoes manage to get hold of several drums of dirty waste oil and pour it into the harbour. In the morning the whole harbour is like a big pool of oil, and any luckless sailors who may have had the idea to paint their boats or dinghies white will discover that the black greasy oil clings to the paint and cannot be removed. Every motorboat that has enough power to raise a wake washes the oil a little higher up the sides of the boats in an irregular wavy line.

A piece of burning twist thrown overboard in a careless moment would turn the whole basin into a sea of flame. It is not pleasant to think what would happen then to all the little wooden boats anchored there and to the petroleum boats alongside the quay, or to the small motorboats with tanks full of petrol. Anyone unlucky enough to fall overboard in the oil may as well go straight to one of the expensive shops kept by the Indians and buy himself a new set of clothes. He won't be able to clean the others.

But that is not all. With muffled oars the Guanchoes row noiselessly round the harbour at night, and, if they find a ship, a newcomer from more peaceable latitudes whose crew in innocent trust in their fellows have omitted to post an armed guard on the deck, they will strip it so that it will be a fortnight at least before it can put to sea again. When daylight comes, halliards and sheets, blocks and compass, direction-finder and anchor-chain, sails and anything else detachable, will have vanished without trace. By that time the Gaunchoes will be over the hills and far away, sitting deep within their inaccessible caves and glee-fully grinning as they divide the spoils of the night.

The first night we spent in Santa Cruz we all turned in when bedtime came. In the early morning the skipper was awakened by something scraping against the door of the deckhouse, and when he opened his trusting blue eyes he saw the silhouette of a half-grown youth busily examining our equipment of nautical instruments. He leaped from his bunk with a roar and our unbidden guest was across the rail in a flash, diving head first into the oil, and swam off rapidly towards a dinghy that was waiting for him in the dark shadow under the stern of an anchored ship.

The jib-halliard had been cut away and taken.

Two drums of costly grease had gone the same way. All the tarpaulins with which the goods stored on deck were covered had been cut through so that our visitor could see what was underneath. A barrel of formalin for preserving zoological specimens had not appealed to our visitors, no doubt because of the smell,

but another of soap had found favour in their eyes.
It was only thanks to the skipper being a light sleeper
that we were not forced to navigate the Atlantic
without sextant, binoculars and all our other expensive
equipment, to say nothing of the fact that we wouldn't
have had a yard of rope or a square foot of sail left.
In fact, we would never have been able to leave Santa
Cruz at all, for prices in this " free " port, where everything is to be had, are so high that those who don't
have dollars in their pocket-books must be content
just to look at the shop windows. If you reckon a
peseta as being worth nearly sixpence, as you must, a
small egg costs a shilling and all other prices are in
proportion.

The following night we mounted a guard, taking it
in turns, two hours at a time. We crouched in the
shadow of the deck-house, thirsting for revenge, and
hoping that the thief or his friends would return to
complete their interrupted visit. We kept watch every
night, but they never came again. It was annoying,
for we were well prepared to receive them had they
come, for we had put a case of fifty bottles of beer by
each rail, and when you take a beer bottle by the neck
it lies in the hand like a grenade and is excellently
designed for close fighting. Also we had two well-
sharpened harpoons on six-foot shafts placed in
readiness. We were really sorry that they never came.

Even so, we lost our battle with the Guanchoes.
Their last act was so barbaric that it will always spoil
my memory of that lovely island. They stole Mette,
our sweet little affectionate mascot, the harum-scarum
kitten we had saved from drowning in the harbour

basin at Copenhagen four months before. Since then we had fed her on plaice from the North Sea, lobster from the English Channel and exotic fish from Lisbon, to say nothing of Portuguese sardines in oil and Norwegian sild in tomato sauce, and liver paste with truffles, and rich oily condensed milk. And they stole her!

It happened after we had begun to keep watch, but how, we shall never know. Some moment during the day or night, when we can't have been looking, someone must have seen their opportunity, stuck a dirty fist over the rail and taken her by the soft scruff of her neck; but whether they drowned her, or sold her, or ate her, we shall never find out. Had she lived, we could have shown her the great wide world.

Those who have never sailed themselves will not be able to understand how much such a little creature can mean on board a small ship. Science no doubt can provide a long psychological explanation of the fact, and will point out that a dog or cat or any other animal among tough men on a lengthy voyage under primitive conditions when they are continually fighting with sea and storms, is a sort of outlet for feelings which they would otherwise be ashamed to express. There is much more behind a heavy hairy hand stroking a little kitten's head than ordinary love of animals, there is a longing for wife and children, or merely for a softer, more gentle life than is the daily lot of the seaman. If you realize that, you will also understand that there is no blasphemy in our saying that we felt as though it was a child we had lost.

Our feelings for Don Juan de Gomera were quite different. Don Juan was a pig, zoologically and in his every act. He would snort derisively into his feeding trough and send his maize and milk showering all over the deck. He was, in fact, a true pig at either end, and also he attracted all the flies in the harbour. We wanted to be rid of him.

It was, of course, tempting to keep him till Christmas, but all the same we felt that we would prefer to gather round a piece of tinned cow or some Bavarian sausages rather than have to slaughter a pig on the high seas. Then another Dane, the S.S. *Dorrit Clausen,* came into harbour. We received a visit from her captain. Yes, Captain Tønnesen thought they had room on the quarter-deck. The cook, it appeared, would be more than willing to cherish Don Juan till Christmas. So we did a swop. *Dorrit* sent us ready cooked pig in the form of hams, shoulders, liver sausage, lard, sausages and other good things, and we sent her the Governor's well-meant, but inconvenient, parting gift. I sincerely hope he will forgive us.

*　　　*　　　*

One evening when the rain was splashing down, we took oil aboard and filled our tanks with fresh water. We were ready to leave this Jekyll and Hyde town that is all pleasantness during the day, but at night turns into a malicious were-wolf. A young man from Fanø, with the sea-fever in his blood, was the only one to see us let the hawsers go and slip away from the quay-side. He was standing under a light on board a tanker lying at the pier-head, and he stood there, alone in the rain, until we could no longer see him.

Three of us went below and drew the blankets over our heads, while the fourth took firm hold of the spokes of the wheel, pulled his sou'wester down over his forehead and watched the black strokes of the compass slowly swinging in the light of the binnacle's sleepy paraffin lamp, until the little thin arrow was pointing west-south-west.

Steady as she goes!

CHAPTER XII

The Long, long Way

From Columbus' Journal:

Thursday, 6th September, 1492: Set sail from the harbour of Gomera this morning and shaped their course for the voyage. The Admiral learnt by a vessel from the island of Ferro that there were three Portuguese caravels cruising about there in search of him. This circumstance probably originated in the envy of the King of Portugal, as the Admiral had left him to resort to Castile. It was calm the whole day and night; in the morning they found themselves between Gomera and Teneriffe.

The sun rose. It was as though the Old World was doing its utmost to make our last impression of it as attractive and charming as possible. The rain had stopped. The sea was lazy and as smooth as oil, softly breathing in a long gentle swell. The deck was still cluttered with the parting gifts given us by the people of Gomera whose mountains and valleys were now merging into one away to starboard, their fine shades of green and brown and red no longer sharp and distinct, but melting into a uniform soft shade of reddish-mauve. Only against the sea and the sky were there any sharp outlines left.

A heavy bunch of bananas hung in the shrouds. Boxes of dates, lemons, oranges, grapes and tomatoes were piled higgledy-piggledy under the dinghy along with others of golden garlic, while in the cupboard in my cabin stood the bottle of clear spring water from the mountains, which the governor had given me at the last moment. It was just ordinary water, he had said, but I was to take it as a symbol, for had not Columbus filled his casks with the self-same water.

Now Gomera lay to starboard, and there astern was Pico de Teide in all its seductive beauty. At that moment the rays of the rising sun caught its top towering in the thin air of 13,000 feet. Even before the sun had appeared above the horizon, the peak had been pink with its early light. Slowly that flush spread downwards across the desolate slopes of grey lava and lit a beacon in the glass window of a lonely cottage near the tree-line. Down and down it crept, peering into the open doors of the houses in the small villages and waking their inhabitants to the joys and sorrows of a new day. Those villages seemed so ridiculously small seen from the sea, just like little patches of mould on the flat uniform expanse of the volcano's sloping side, for at that distance the furrows in the lava were no longer visible.

Ahead of us lay Hierro, the most southerly of the Canary Islands; astern and to larboard the shadow of Gran Canarie was outlined against a sky that grew brighter and brighter as we watched. Far away in the gap between Teneriffe and Gomera we could just make out the hazy outline of Palma. The Canaries were all there to bid us farewell.

From the north-east came the Trades, at first like stealthy cat's paws stealing across a rosy-coloured sea, then, in mischievous gusts that set the foresail fluttering, and, finally, when the whole orange disc of the sun stood clear of the horizon, they came blowing with uniform strength filling the sails and making the water gurgle round our sharp white bows.

Slowly *Santa Maria* glided westwards in between Gomera and Hierro. The islanders, when they flung open their shutters and went out to their day's work in the banana plantations and tomato fields, can scarcely have noticed the little white fleck out there on the sea, a fleck that was a boat sailing alone to a rendezvous with adventure and carrying but four men aboard.

Evening came, and then it was night. And the following morning we were alone in the sea and the dawn.

Saturday, 8th September 1492; At three in the afternoon the wind rose from the N.E. Steered their course W., encountered a strong head sea, which impeded their progress. Sailed day and night, nine leagues.

And a hard night awaited us. There must presumably have been a storm somewhere away to the north, for that evening huge waves suddenly came swooping down and made *Maria* roll heavily with flapping sails. After that the wind came and filled foresail and mainsail so suddenly and so fiercely that we had to reef them immediately, for the lee rail was running under water and the peak of the main boom ploughing deep furrows in the waves to port. In the gathering darkness we could see the occasional gleam of a white watery fang, and every now and again a spatter of spray would sweep like smoke across the rail. The water was washing backwards and forwards across the deck until, spluttering, it found its way back to the sea through the open scuppers.

The jib-boom dipped under water. As we stood there watching the bows, it seemed an eternity before it began to rise; but then it emerged out of the dark waters, shook itself like a dog just out of the sea, and cocked itself up steeply to point at what stars were visible between the coursing clouds. Meanwhile the water was foaming round the skylight and companion as it made its way aft, where the mizzen outhauler boom was in its turn burying itself in the sea along with half the stern. The man at the wheel was standing up to his waist in water that swirled round his bare legs.

" I want to go ashore," said Niels.

" And so you will," I answered. " Land is only 3.000 miles away."

And so *Santa Maria* reeled on into the darkness.

There was no rest to be had in our bunks. *Maria* was rolling and pitching, and every lurch seemed to be trying to throw us out over the edge. Then the table in the saloon broke loose and set off on its own, waddling from side to side, till we had to get up in our bare feet and catch it in full career, like cowboys wrestling with a frantic steer. There was no time to screw it down again, nor the tools to hand, so we had to wedge it between the chest seats as best we could and creep back into our bunks to wait for daylight, listening to the water hissing and gurgling on the other side of the hull, just an inch of pine planking away.

From time to time a wave would come, bigger than the rest, and dash against the boat's side, so that *Maria* halted in her course, heeled over and quivered like a nervous horse. Lying there in our bunks we could feel the groaning planks give slightly at the joints, feel how the stern was squeezed out of alignment for an instant before returning to its former position until the next blow came. The blocks creaked, the sheets hammered against the rail and were stretched taut with violent jerks, but *Maria* sailed on towards the west.

I lay in my bunk seeing our boat as the vessel must have appeared out there in the darkness, a solitary speck of white in a sea the colour of night, so small as scarcely to be distinguishable from the foam on top of the waves. Mentally I compared her size with the immensity of the Atlantic Ocean, her strength with the weight of water in the waves dealing blow upon blow at her side. Occasionally my heart would stand still for a moment, and into my mind's eye would come a picture of a growling bear with a fragile match-box clasped in his heavy paws. And the bear would play with it, patting it this way and that, rolling it round and tossing it from paw to paw. Of course for the bear it was only an amusing game, but who knew when he would strike it a real blow?

Anyone who says that he is not afraid in a storm is a liar. Either that, or he is quite devoid of imagination and incapable of seeing the bear and the box of matches. But should he say that, despite his fears, he *likes* a storm at sea, he may well be telling the truth. You see, out of one's fears grows the urge to survive; and there is the deep satisfaction for a modern man to discover that he is in a situation where for once he must think and act on his own, without having to ask permission or to fill in forms in triplicate before he does anything. That and something of primitive man's childish, rather fearful joy at holding his life in his own hands, like something small and warm, and knowing that what he does is spared any superfluous formalities. That is a feeling that makes you forget a few moments of fear.

Maria ploughed on her way until morning came and with it a sun that rose up red astern. At that, the wind died away as suddenly as it had come. Then the booms banged to and fro across the deck, and we hurriedly had to haul them amidships and make the sheets properly fast; for if you get in the way of a main boom when it is threshing like that, it can kill you. But then the seas subsided as well. We had now taken final leave of the North.

After that, the Trades came stealthily back and filled our sails again with a whispered apology for the rough-and-tumble of the previous night. When the sun was round and whole above the horizon, we picked up a little flying fish that had landed on the deck in the dark, and as we looked aloft, up at the truck, we caught sight of a snow-white tropical bird with long beautiful tailfeathers. It circled down over the boat and dropped its visiting card on to the roof of the wheel-house.

Our first flying-fish and our first tropical bird!

Maria heeled gently, almost caressingly, over on the port bow and sped westwards, running from the gentle Trades as a girl runs from her lover.

Sunday, 16th September, 1942. The admiral here says that from this time they experienced very pleasant weather, and that the mornings were most delightful, wanting nothing but the melody of the nightingale. He compares the weather to that of Andalusia in April.

And so it was day after day. Monotonous? Maybe the harassed townsman with his thirst for change would have called it that and paced restlessly back and forth across the narrow deck, or sat in the cabin drumming his fingers on the shiny surface of the mahogany table. So many people imagine that you cannot do without the morning papers, the wireless's recitals of disaster and the telephone's ringing. They cannot, perhaps. When they try, they are usually restless and unhappy. About such people there is nothing to be done. The tempo of the twentieth century has poisoned their blood.

How could anyone talk of monotony here, where all day long great clouds are drifting slothfully along the horizon, where sunrise and sunset are always miracles of beauty and diversity and never the same; where the whole vault of the sky and the expanse of the sea is turned each morning and evening into a lovely cathedral of such compelling beauty that even the most arrant heathen is forced into devout silence during those long seconds when a new day is being created or passing away. At such moments sea and sky reward you richly for enduring their dark nights of storm and grim grey days.

How can you say nothing happens, when flying fish are leaping at short intervals, sailing out of one wave, like a silver arrow from the bow of some playful mermaid to pierce the heart of another in a scurry of spray; or when graceful shiny dolphins are crotcheting intricate patterns of white and blue in front of the boat's bows, until, suddenly, some whim makes them abandon their game and set off for the horizon in great tumbler's leaps so far above the water that you can catch the white glint of their bellies?

Follow the squalls on their way round the horizon, or go for'ard in the warm calm night, lean over the rail and make yourself spectator of the fireworks of the phosphorescence with its bursts of different size and changing colour in the white cascade of the bow waves. Close your eyes, put your head back and fill your lungs with air that has never been contaminated with dust or with smoke from a factory chimney. You will then realize that the Trades can be as enchanting as Andalusia in April.

And there won't be a ship to be seen all round the horizon; for you are far off the steamship routes, and the proud big sailing ships that a hundred years ago made the belt of the Trades the great convoy route of the seas have long since folded their wings and now are lying tucked away and forgotten in dirty harbours, where they serve as humble store-ships for the coal the busy black steamers need, those dirty tramps that have taken on their job but not given us any of their beauty and poetry.

The world progresses, doesn't it?

However, our bows were pointed at the sinking sun and what we saw each evening was just what Columbus had seen. Here the centuries have brought no change. Long, gentle rollers; large lazy cumulus drifting clouds which the last rays of the sun gild and transform into bricks with which imagination builds. The Trades are as timeless as the sea and as the clouds of the heavens. And the sound of the sea gurgling round the bows, its chuckling in the wake, are the same to-day as they were on 10th September, 1492.

CHAPTER XIII

The Swarming Sargasso

FROM COLUMBUS' JOURNAL :

Saturday, 15*th* 1492 : *Sailed day and night, W. twenty-seven leagues and more. In the beginning of the night saw a remarkable bolt of fire fall into the sea at the distance of four or five leagues.*

"Get up! Get up and put some clothes on!" shouted Jens, brutally dragging the blankets off me.

I gazed dazedly at the phosphorescent hands of the clock. According to them it was four-thirty : an extremely brutal hour to be awakened. Anyway what was up? Had he seen land? Were we on the point of sinking? Or had the loneliness just got on his nerves? But Jens was already back at the wheel.

I pulled on my shorts. The thick panes of the sky-light were grey with the first pale light of day. As I reached the deck, I saw that Jens was standing with his back turned gazing astern towards the faint glow that heralded the dawn. Then, suddenly, I was wide awake, for there in the eastern sky, low down near the horizon, was a comet trailing a fiery streak behind it. The glow of the rising sun had bleached it, but it was still distinct with shining head and sweeping tail of hazy light.

Niels, who had only just fallen asleep after his spell at the wheel, now stuck his tousled head out of his hammock and blinked at the light. His mouth opened

to curse his disturber, but the oath never came, for
Niels had seen the comet. He was only twenty-seven,
and neither he nor Jens had had an opportunity of
seeing such a phenomenon before. (I can still remember the tremendous impression Brook's comet
made upon me when I saw it in 1911.) Then the
skipper came and looked and asked whether that was
all. It was scarcely worth waking him for, he said.
He, of course, had seen much bigger comets often
enough. And so we discussed the comet till the sun
had risen and smothered it.

A comet! Now, supposing it had rammed the
earth in the western hemisphere, it would have been
quite possible that the West Indies and the entire New
World would have disappeared by the time we got
there. Of course, we would have been able to write quite
sensational articles about our discovery of nothing,
but it would have destroyed the whole original idea
of the voyage. Or, if it had rammed the earth behind
us, Europe might have been so badly damaged that
there would have been no readers for the book I used
to sit there thumping out on a typewriter that leaped
about the swaying table like a frisky foal. Again,
if it had fallen into the sea somewhere between the
new and old worlds, would *Maria* have been able to
outride the tidal wave it would obviously have set up?
However we looked at it, we could see little hope
for ourselves, so we just prayed that on this occasion
too the comet would pass clear of the earth, that it was
a friendly comet that had just come to draw a parallel
between Columbus' voyage and ours.

There was, indeed, more than one such parallel.

Here is Columbus' journal for 17th September:

Monday, 17th September, 1492: Steered W. and sailed day and night, about fifty leagues; They saw a great deal of weed which proved to be rock-weed, it came from the W. and they met with it very frequently . . . At dawn they saw many more weeds, apparently river weeds, and among them a live crab, which the admiral kept, and says that these are sure signs of land, being never found eighty leagues out at sea. They found the sea-water less salt since they left the Canaries, and the air more mild. They were all very cheerful . . .

Eleven days out from Gomera, Columbus met with the first of the drifting sea-grass. Eleven days out from Gomera, we saw the first yellowish clumps of Sargasso seaweed; but we did not excite ourselves with optimistic calculations of the nearness of land as Columbus had done, for during the centuries in between our two voyages scientists of all countries have been busy trying to solve the puzzle of the Sargasso Sea, and we now know that this strange huge expanse of seaweed, that is kept in its place in the middle of the Atlantic by currents that patrol the periphery, has no connection with land.

It is to be supposed that once in the morning of time the original seaweed was rooted to the coast of the New World; then some of it drifted out to sea and learned to dispense with contact with the floor of the ocean, discovered how to extract its nourishment from the sea itself and from the air, and ever since it has grown and expanded independently of the land.

This strange area of seaweed stretches between roughly the twentieth and fortieth degree North and from the thirty-fifth to the seventy-fifth degree west. The seaweed is thickest in the middle of this great expanse of water, where it sometimes lies in great strips so long, broad and dense, that you see more seaweed than water. Its density in these parts has given rise to many of the sailor's tales of ships that have stuck fast in it and drifted round and round until, with a crew of skeletons, they have ended up in the very centre, where the naked masts of hundreds of dead ships form a macabre forest.

But then the steamer came, and before long aeroplanes were speeding across the Sargasso Sea. It was found that there were no dead ships, not even any hindrances to prevent a ship sailing through. The layer of seaweed was thin and the screws of the steamers cut through it easily, while their crews hauled up buckets of water and found the small crabs which Columbus took as a sure sign of the immediate neighbourhood of land.

The microscope has revealed many fantastic facts about the creepy-crawly life that exists among the drifting seaweed; and it was a Dane, Professor Johannes Schmidt, on his expedition there in the *Dana* who solved the problem of where the eel breeds.  Till then this had been shrouded in the deepest mystery and his discovery was of as much significance as though he had caught the great sea-serpent itself. What he discovered was that each year the eels leave the watercourses and narrow fjords of Europe and deliberately make the long trip to the Sargasso Sea where they breed and die. Then the transparent eel larvae set off on their way back to their parent's home

and during the course of that long trip they develop
into the small persistent baby eels that in each spring
swarm up from the sea into our brooks, lakes and fjords.

Into this breeding ground of the eels we were now
sailing. Every day saw the strips of seaweed growing
denser and denser. At times they ran from east to west,
at others from north to south, it all depended on the
direction of the winds. We got out a net and made
our own investigations, sampling every clump of
seaweed with the eager intentness of a monkey picking
over a companion. We were richly rewarded for our
curiosity and labour. There *were* animals, animals in
every clump of seaweed however small : tiny shrimps
less than a centimetre long and crabs in the same
proportion that would run sideways across the deck
in utter bewilderment. Less often, when we shook
the seaweed, out would come a larger crab an inch
or more long that with a lightning movement would
stab your finger with its thin pointed claw and draw
blood.

It was more amusing when we fished up a clump
that contained a dozen or more transversely striped
needle fish ranging from two to six inches in length,
or a single fantastic toad-fish with fingers on its fins and
an extraordinarily stupid expression on its face. The
great event was when we hauled up a " real " tropical
fish ablaze with colours.

Each species was segrated and the various specimens
quickly found their way into our jars of formalin;
but that was later—not at the beginning. Then, still
being novices at marine research, we just used to pick
the creatures out of the seaweed and put them all

together in a bucket to be sorted later in the day. However, it sometimes happened that by the time we returned to it, there would be only a single crab or toad-fish to sort, the rest of all that swarming life having been eaten by the one who was the fittest and had the greatest appetite. None respected another. Large toad-fish ate small toad-fish, and large crabs small crabs. In fact, the creatures of the Sargasso Sea were not a whit better than us humans. The needle-fish and shrimps seemed to be the only decent ones and never attacked their neighbours, but then of course they have no means of defending themselves so they were hardly likely to engage in broils. The result of all this was that we had to inform the museum for which we were collecting specimens, that we were sending it a large number of shrimps and other small fry packed in some large crabs which they would have to dissect and sort out for themselves.

The Sargasso was a welcome change in our daily life, especially for our two fishermen, Niels and Jens, who were soon talking of good and lesser " casts " just as though they were once more trawling in the North Sea. They it was who could never make up their minds whether flying fish, " those bastard crosses between swallows and sticklebacks," were to be considered fish or birds.

There is an old belief that you can catch flying fish by hanging up a lantern at night so that its light shines on the mainsail. The flying fish are then supposed to fly towards the light, as migrating birds do towards a lighthouse. We tried this, for we wanted some flying fish for the Zoological Museum.

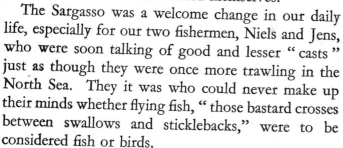

For three nights in succession we flood-lit the main-sail, dazzling the man at the wheel so badly that he would never have been able to see the *Queen Mary* had she come along. But we never caught a single flying fish. Then we gave up the attempt and after that our unlit ship's lanterns were the only light on board at night. The result was that during the next few nights we caught several flying fish. Now, this tale of the attraction of light for flying fish I am inclined to consign along with other such myths to the ship's graveyard in the Sargasso Sea. One day, I shall write a thesis about this for my B.Sc.

Saturday, 22nd September, 1942: Steered about W.N.W. Varying their course, and making thirty leagues' progress. Saw few weeds. Some pardelas were seen, and another bird. The Admiral here says, "This head wind was very necessary to me, for my crew had grown much alarmed, dreading that they should never meet in these seas with a fair wind to return to Spain."

Sunday, 23rd September 1492: Saw a turtle dove, a pelican, a river bird, and other white fowl,—weeds in abundance with crabs among them. The sea being smooth and tranquil, the sailors murmured . . .

Sargasso weed is not a thing that can hold the ordinary person's interest for eight days at a stretch. Before long we had grown rather fastidious and refused even to look at anything that was really tiny. Niels and Jens even said that they were gradually growing rather bored with the proceedings. At that I rubbed my hands, hoping that events were going to follow Columbus' journal so exactly that we too were going to see mutiny on board our *Santa Maria*. I

The submarine world of the coral

Long Island : the white church the priest built with his own hands, and one of the negroes' wretched huts

imagined the crew crowding round me, growling and menacing, and threatening to throw me overboard if I didn't produce land for them within two days. But we had no need of mutiny, for as it was, our log was to put Columbus' journal in the shade.

We were lying right in the middle of the Atlantic. It was a pitch-black night, the time three a.m. It was Niel's watch and the rest of us were snoring in our bunks. Suddenly I was awakened by an earsplitting hullaballoo: it sounded as though Neptune himself had picked up a club and was hammering away on our starboard side in an attempt to smash poor *Santa Maria*. I raced up on deck.

We had been caught by a violent squall and were lying well over on the starboard bow. The water was pouring over the leeward rail and foaming towards the scuppers, while the rain streamed down. The aftermost chainplate of the mainmast had snapped through with the pressure. Chainplate? You don't know what the chainplate is! You know what a shroud is? Not even that! Well, I take it you know what a mast is? All right. Well, the mast is supported on either side by some steel ropes stretching to the rail, which keeps it from falling into the water. These ropes are fixed to a piece of iron set in the ship's side and extending from the rail to the water line. These are the chainplates.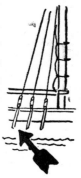

Well, the chainplate was swinging backwards and forwards and the shroud was quite slack. My first thought was, "Thank goodness it wasn't the leeward chainplate that had broken, otherwise the mainmast might easily have gone with it." I called the others

E 129

and, after reefing in the mainsail as far as it would go, we managed to secure everything at least temporarily. We did that in the pitch darkness.

Having got over that, the exhaust pipe amidships caught fire. The flames hissed and spurted several feet up into the air—up to where the mainsail was. And, of course, the mainsail caught fire. Dry, tightly stretched sailcloth burns well and quickly. Luckily, Jens was on the spot with a bucket, and thanks to his quickness and presence of mind the flames were put out almost at once and we were still able to use the sail, for only the foot-lining and a bit of the bolt rope were burned.

In the morning we set about passing a thick hawser under the keel, so that the broken chainplate had the support of the whole one on the other side. That done, the skipper got out his needle, thread and thimble and sat down to patch the mainsail. Then as we sat round the table enjoying our afternoon coffee and a welcome rest, water began quietly trickling up under our feet. We tore up the man-hole trap and from what we saw it looked as though we were on the point of sinking. The water was well above all our bottles and the labels had soaked off, so that ever afterwards we were never able to tell what sort of beer we would get when we fished out a bottle.

The pump wouldn't pump as the feed-pipe was choked with pulpy beer labels. Just as we got that cleared and the pump working, the sun went down.

Not wishing to omit any of the circumstances of that eventful day, I may mention that it was our thirteenth out from the Canaries.

CHAPTER XIV

A World Emerges

FROM COLUMBUS' JOURNAL:

Saturday, 29th September 1492 : The air was soft and refreshing, and the Admiral says nothing was wanting but the singing of the nightingale; the sea as smooth as a river . . .

Sunday, 30th September : . . . Four tropic birds came to the ship which is a very clear sign of land, for so many birds of one sort together show that they are not straying about, having lost themselves. Twice, saw two pelicans, many weeds . . .

A dead-white tropical bird with long graceful tail-feathers circled our mainmast head for a long time, and made repeated attempts to settle on the truck. We watched it with bated breath and got our cameras ready. It is very seldom that this, the most beautiful bird of the tropic seas, ever deigns to settle on a ship to rest. Ours, too, after several vain attempts gave up and flew away.

We did not let ourselves be misled by its presence, as Columbus had been. We could look at our chart and see that we were in the middle of the Atlantic, and to-day we know that tropical birds go much farther from land than Columbus ever suspected. But then, of course, Columbus was anxiously on the lookout for any sign that might indicate the proximity of land; nor can he be blamed for that, having as he did, a crew that fear and impatience had made mutinous, and a second-in-command who thought he knew better than his chief. To his persistence Columbus eventually yielded and altered course, steering south-west, with the result that he discovered a few poor insignificant islands, instead of landing on the main-land at what is now the coast of Florida, as he would have done had he maintained the course he had all along been steering.

My crew never thought of mutiny, which would rather point to those who doubt whether Columbus' ever did being right. As a matter of fact, the skipper's face was even beginning to lengthen just because we were drawing near to land. He hates the land. Then, when we were 800 miles east of San Salvador some-thing happened that would have rejoiced Columbus' heart; Niels saw a butterfly. It was a real butterfly, a lovely reddish-brown butterfly fluttering gaily round the boat. It must have hatched out on board, the pupa presumably having found its way aboard in some basket of fruit that we got in the Canaries.

Some mornings later, when *Santa Maria* was drifting round with no way on her and sails hanging slack, a graceful little swallow suddenly came flying out of the blue and perched on the rail, where it sat with its head on one side and black eyes blinking. At that moment the nearest land was 700 miles away! Columbus would at once have sent a man up into the rigging to have a look for it, but we knew better. Had that swallow been blown off its course by a storm on its long flight from North to South across the Caribbean? Or had it stowed away on some steamer and been carried far out to sea? We shall never know.

As soon as it was feeling rested, the swallow disappeared as it had come. Let us hope that it reached land.

Columbus regarded the birds he saw as portents and was cheated every time. We were cleverer and more sceptical; and we had our chart and our instruments. But all the same we kept an eye open for any sign, that might foreshadow the end of our long voyage, and for any hint of the New World that was to appear right ahead of the sprit.

A sailor's life is sometimes a queer mixture of emancipation and duty, of unconcern and excitement, and so it was with us now. Also, when he hasn't seen a newspaper for three weeks, he becomes most inquisitive. But I am anticipating.

Thursday, 11th October, 1492: . . . Saw pardelas and a green rush near the vessel. The crew of the Pinta saw a cane and a log; they also picked up a stick which appeared to have been carved with an iron tool, a piece of cane, a plant which grows on land, and a board. The crew of the Niña saw other signs of land, and a stalk loaded with roseberries . . .

There it was, drifting along with lazy nonchalance, as though it were an everyday occurrence for a bottle to be floating out in the Atlantic. We put the helm hard over and fished it up. The upper part was covered with barnacles; the cork was in, but the bottle was empty. We were on the point of throwing it back into the sea, when I noticed that there was raised lettering on one side of the bottle. " Pedro Domeque " it spelt. Pedro Domeque, the best name in Spanish brandy; better known in the Spanish-speaking countries of the world then **Hennessey**, Martell, and Courvoisier are in the North.

So it was a Spanish bottle! And had not Columbus got his provisions in the south of Spain where, at Jerez de la Frontera, Pedro Domeque is made? Perhaps, the monks at Rabida had given Columbus a bottle or two, or the alcalde of Palos sent Pinzon off with a case? We decided that we would keep the bottle and sell it to a museum at home. Why not? Round about the world there are at least about a dozen anchors that are said to have belonged to *Santa Maria*; Columbus is buried in three or four places; he was born in seven different Italian towns to say nothing of Corsica; so why shouldn't we have the only brandy bottle thrown overboard from the *Santa Maria* in 1492 and picked up by the *Santa Maria* in 1948? There are plenty of tales about objects that have drifted about the seas for countless years before being picked up. All the same I do wish that Columbus had put a note inside.

The following day we saw a piece of **cork**. It had a groove in the middle and was a float fishermen use to keep their nets up. An hour or two later, a tree came drifting along, a well-grown tree with branches, twigs and green leaves which had hardly withered at all. A small turtle was swimming in and out of the branches.

It was obvious that land was close. Going into the chart-house we saw that, unless our reckoning was all wrong, it was less than a hundred miles away. With the Trades blowing as freshly as they then were, that meant that we should reach it in from twelve to fifteen hours and sight it long before.

Friday, 12th October, 1492: . . .as the Pinta was the swiftest sailor, and kept ahead of the Admiral, she discovered land and made the signals which had been ordered. The land was first seen by a sailor called Rodrigo de Triana . .

With us it was Niels Underbjerg from Tørring who first saw land, having for the last few days spent most of his free watches up aloft. Columbus had offered a silken jacket to whoever first saw land and the king and queen of Spain a reward of an annuity of ten thousand *maravedis*. So, following their example I had promised to who ever first reported land ahead, ten U.S.A. dollars in brand new notes. We had arrived at dollars by way of compromise. In the first place, I neither possessed, nor knew where to buy any maravedis, and we doubted whether they would have been accepted as legal tender on the other side; then, my crew swore that nothing would ever make them wear a silken jacket.

Knowing how many false alarms there had been on board the original *Santa Maria*, we had decided that anyone reporting land ahead, when there was none, should be fined two dollars a time. As a result we were very careful and gazed suspiciously at many a low grey cloud on the horizon, but without opening our mouths. So, when Niels roared out " Land ahead to starboard," it *was* land.

It is one thing to strike a continent at some chance spot, as Columbus did, but another to hit a certain island on a certain degree of latitude and longitude after taking aim at it from somewhere in the Canary Islands and then sailing for twenty-five days without ever seeing land. It is all the more of a feat when all you have is a wind and current chart on which it is printed that it cannot be used for navigation, and when your compasses have one leg loose and your chronometer is an old turnip watch that sometimes loses and sometimes gains a couple of minutes in the twenty-four hours.

However, there was land, first a lighthouse, tall and white; then, half-an-hour later a long fringe appeared in the west. It now looked as though there were two islands, which wouldn't have been right, but it was really just one island with a dip in the middle : San Salvador.

Niels went below and fetched an old German rifle which he had filched whilst disarming Hitler's army in Jutland, and fired a salute of six shots. Then we drank a glass of wine, and Niels himself extracted the ten dollars out of my pocket book.

SANTA MARIA

We drew nearer the island. It looked appallingly dreary, and not in the least exotic or romantic : a few low light-coloured cliffs with some dull green dwarf plants on top, a white strip of foam marking where a reef stretched along the whole of the east coast. Here, the *Chicago Tribune* has erected a solemn memorial to inform the world that on that spot Columbus for the first time trod American soil. You have to laugh. I suppose some two or three hundred people may have seen it, but there cannot have been many more who have. I can only imagine that it was the editor of the housewife's page or the agricultural correspondent, who got the idea when one day glancing through his son's school atlas. If they had had a chart in the office or taken the trouble to visit the place before deciding to put up their monument, they would have realized that any sailor who chose to go ashore at that spot, must have been both mad and drunk, and his entire crew must have been in chains, otherwise they would have prevented him.

Along the whole length of the east coast runs a coral reef, a really nasty one. The rusty skeletons of steamers, large and small, bear witness to its treachery. We would not have dared attempt a landing even in calm weather, for there is always surf breaking over the low reef and the sea-bottom is coveredwith jagged sharp coral rocks of the dreaded kind that rise like towers out of deep water. The chart is as thickly covered with crosses in that part as is a churchyard, and every cross marks a dangerous rock.

No, Columbus was cleverer than that. He had come a long way and he wasn't in such a tremendous hurry that he could not have waited a little longer, now that he had discovered land. The land would not have run away, even though he did prowl a bit round the island under a reduced spread of canvas, looking for a safe spot. I am willing to bet that he did exactly what we did.

We didn't know where Columbus had landed. In fact, I understand that nobody does for sure. But, after a look at the chart, we stood south round the island, got in lee of the ocean swell, slipped round the low sandy south-westerly point and crept up the west coast in the lee of low-lying land, but still beyond and out of reach of the reef that we could see as a dark strip in the blue sea. Inside it, the lagoon was green with dark patches: rocks on a sandy bottom.

Somewhere, halfway up the west coast, the reef
suddenly stopped. There was no longer a dark line
dividing the blue and the green; the latter began where
the former stopped, and the shore that ran south from
a little insignificant village with a wireless mast and a
house of pink bricks, was a stretch of lovely gleaming
white sand. I'll take my oath that Columbus was just
as delighted as we at the sight of that lovely beach
lying there sheltered from the ocean swell and the
Trades. And that he did exactly what we did, you can
read in his journal :

*. . . the Admiral landed in the boat, which was armed,
along with Martin Alonzo Pinzon, and Vincent Janez his
brother, Captain of the Niña. The Admiral bore the royal
standard, and the two captains each a banner of the Green
Cross, which all the ships had carried. . .*

Our skipper put on his white peaked cap, twirled
his moustache, and went ashore in the boat, accompanied by Jens Larsen Underbjerg and his brother,
Niels. In his hand the skipper bore a fine paper Danish
flag, and he was just going to plant it in the white
sand when a whole crowd of people came running
along the shore and one of them stepped up and said :

"Who are you? May I see your passports? Is
your Customs manifest in order? And how dare you
go ashore when the quarantine officials have not even
been on board!"

I told him that we had come straight from Europe,
that the voyage had taken longer than the three weeks
required by the quarantine regulations, that we were
following Columbus' route and had come the whole
way in the little boat he could see out there. Then I

noticed that the man—a very black man—was wearing an alpaca jacket and that he had ink on his fingers, so I knew that it was hopeless. There was nothing about Columbus in his rules and instructions. The skipper rolled up his paper flag and we went back to the boat and rowed out to *Maria* to prepare for a second landing through the labyrinth of statutory rules and red tape.

It was the constable who had thus upset our plan for making a landing worthy of the occasion. To tell the truth, he was really a very decent chap, considering the power he wielded as the one and only representative of government in that village of 137 inhabitants. Only, you had to be very careful of his honour and to avoid interfering in the exercise of his official functions, as I did some days later. Another of the duties entrusted to him was that of the island's postman. I made the mistake of trying to help him in that difficult task. I wished to send an air mail letter which ought to have carried six sixpenny stamps. The constable-postman got out paper and pencil and proceeded to calculate the sum total. Seeing that he was finding this difficult, I told him that it was 36 pence, or three shillings. At that, he gave me such a dirty look over the top of his spectacles, that I did not dare utter another word. In the end, the letter was despatched carrying stamps to the value of 24 pence, and it did reach its destination—but not by air mail.

I never succeeded in gaining that man's confidence. As far as he was concerned, I was suspect. One evening several days later I suggested to the island's Catholic priest that I should show the islanders a film they had never seen before. The news of this spread, and the next time I went ashore there stood the constable, black and menacing, demanding that I accompany him at once to the Governor's office.

" Did I not know," he enquired, " that the correct thing to do, was to make such or similar proposals to the highest authority in the island and not to run with them to any Tom, Dick or Harry? "

From this I concluded that the constable belonged either to the Church of England or to the Baptists. I dutifully went to the governor and we did show the film; but that is another story.

The credit for the show went to the Catholic priest, which pleased me, for he was a very nice man. He patched our rubber boat and sold us two fat chickens. He was one of those priests who are always experimenting with things. When I knew him, he was investigating the mysteries of electricity and used to put out small lumps of meat for his neighbour's dogs, which gave them a slight electric shock whenever they opened their jaws to seize a morsel. That was the sort of man Father Nicholas was.

He really was a nice man, and he was enchanted when I told him that the large cross put up just where we had gone ashore, had been set there to mark the actual spot at which Columbus had landed. It hadn't, of course. It was the rallying point for the Catholic cemetery, but we told him that he could safely inform people that it was there that the priests in Columbus' train had set up the first cross ever planted in the New World.

That ought to annoy my friend, the constable; if only because I did not make the suggestion to the Governor.

In the evening, having complied with all the formalities, we rowed ashore again, planted our paper flag in the sand in front of the cross and took possession of the island in the name of the Royal House of Denmark. I hope the flag is still standing there.

(I know that San Salvador really forms part of the British Empire under the heading Bahama Islands; but you British have so many little islands—and I did want to take possession of our first one. Only, not a word about it to the constable. Heaven knows, what he would say or do.)

CHAPTER XV

The Truth about San Salvador

Now, the truth shall out. It can no longer harm Columbus. Ferdinand and Isabella are long since dead, and the Spaniards have other things with which to occupy their minds. Let me first say, though, that I do understand and entirely sympathize with my dear colleague, Christopher.

Before he started on the voyage there was no end to the wonderful things he promised to find on the other side for Isabella and her rather sulky husband, for he had to keep her up to scratch and see that the royal purse-strings remained loosened. He did it beautifully. He got his three caravels and his crews, and the royal couple agreed to all his conditions about dividends, royalties, titles and gold chains. So, when he reached his goal to see those islands emerge out of the October night and finally landed and took possession of them, what else could he do but describe them as wonderful, fairy-tale lands with " trees very green, many streams of water, and diverse sorts of fruit." And, of course, there had to be " a  king who possessed large vessels of gold, and in great quantities; " and there were " groves of trees, the most beautiful I have ever seen, with their foliage as verdant as we see in Castile in April and May."

You see, he had to write that sort of thing. He could never have forced himself to admit that seen from the sea the island was flat and dreary, that it did not have a single watercourse, just a few salt lakes in its centre, in which even fish couldn't exist; that it was a poor place compared with the loveliness of the Andalusia he had left and of which he was always writing in his journal. He could never have written that in a letter home.

Nature has treated the southern islands of the Bahamas like the traditional stepmother. My description of them is much shorter than Columbus'; they are hot, dry, stinkingly poor, and swarming with sandflies.

SAN SALVADOR

The Indians called the island Guanahani. Try speaking it slowly, Gu-a-na-ha-ni, and you will realize what a pretty name it is, a soft, pleasing name, that is rather reminiscent of a child's first attempts to talk. Columbus called it San Salvador, for those were pious days. When the English snapped up the islands after the Spaniards had abandoned them, having found fatter lands to exploit farther on, they re-named it Watling Island after a certain Mr. Watling who was a notorious pirate. Since then, pious folk in England have had its original name restored and it is now officially called San Salvador, though all charts and most atlases still show it under Mr. Watling's name.

The highest point in the island is forty-eight feet above sea-level; the greatest depth in the salt lakes in its centre, sixteen feet. There isn't a good reliable harbour in the island and you must always be ready to raise anchor should the wind veer round, as it quite often does. What the island does possess, is several miles of magnificent bathing beaches, untrodden stretches of reddish-golden coral sand as fine as flour, shelving into water so gleaming pure and emerald that you cannot resist the temptation to throw off your clothes and dive in. If you do that, don't come up again! Keep below the surface! The moment you let your head or a shoulder emerge out of the water, the sandflies will fall upon it like ravening wolves. You can't see them. You can't hear them. They are so small that no mosquito-net can keep them out, but they bite like bulldogs and inject a caustic poison into the wound, that makes your skin swell into a lump bigger than any midge-bite and which itches much worse.

There are only 143 families on the island. There used to be many more, but San Salvador is the island of despair and those of its inhabitants who can get away, disappear to the U.S.A. and take jobs on the cotton and tobacco plantations of the southern states. The island is far from self-supporting. It has to have a subsidy from the Government, which it receives largely in the form of grants for roads and other public works that alone keep the islanders from sinking into a state of complete apathy. Their fare is wretched, containing not a half of the vitamins they need, so that nutritional diseases and mental disorders are the most common ills of its primitive population. The Government also has to assist in supporting the families of the emigrants to the tune of some £800 a year.

The negroes burn a patch of the bush, a bush out of which no tall trees rise towering to the skies, and in among the charred stumps they plant a handful of maize, a few beans, some groundnuts and sweet potatoes, just what is essential to maintain life for those who don't believe in vitamins. They have tried pineapples, but there is too much work involved; and the few orange and lemon trees that there are, are becoming old and degenerating. What little fruit is to be got from them is small. The goats, sheep and dogs are languishing away, growing smaller and weaker with every new generation because of inter-breeding. It rains a little in April-June and September-November, but during the rest of the year not a drop falls. Then, the heat is fierce and everything burned up. The negroes sit apathetically and lethargically in front of their huts. There are few who can be bothered even to fish.

That is the truth about San Salvador.

The English planters left the island the moment slavery was abolished. The remains of their magnificent houses, with slave quarters and imposing drives, are still there. The slaves received them as a gift along with their freedom; yet they have been let go to rack and ruin.

In 1492 this little island was floodlit by the interest of the whole world. But that is long since over and done with. To-day, when the sun goes down into the sea, the people of San Salvador go to bed behind hermetically closed doors and shuttered windows. None can afford to burn expensive paraffin. You will only see two lights burning : one in the priest's study; the other in a stable lantern tied to a post down by the "harbour." The sailing handbooks call it "unreliable"—and with every justification. Had any

ships come to the island by night whilst we were there, they would have steered straight for *Santa Maria's* anchor light which could be seen at a much greater distance than the harbour-light, and so they would have run on to the reef. However, seldom if ever does an unexpected ship come to the island. The only one to come, indeed, is the post-boat. It arrives once every fortnight with newspapers and official correspondence for the priest, wireless-operator and Governor. The wireless-operator had ample time for reading his paper, as the wireless station had broken down and Heaven alone knew when he would ever get the spare parts he needed. And anyway, what on earth was there to send wireless messages about?

There is no doctor on the island. A coal-black woman acts as midwife, and the nearest hospital is in Nassau, two days' sail away.

The Governor, or the Commissioner, as is his official title, is a coal-black gentleman of between thirty and thirty-five. He takes his office very seriously and wears a tie and collar all day. He and his wife have done a great deal to improve conditions in the island. They have personally taught the people how to bottle fruit and vegetables. They got hold of four preserving  pans and four primus stoves which are now stationed round about the island, as a sort of co-operative venture in giving the islanders with their crazy diet, the possibility of benefiting from their fruits and vegetables out of season. On his tours of inspection the Commissioner chugs along on the only motor-bicycle in the island. Either that or he borrows the priest's car. There are only three motors on the island : a station car, a hoary lorry, and the priest's aged Ford which is kept together by wire and adhesive tape.

The priest also does what he can to improve conditions. His great aim is to get the people to drink goat's milk, which is healthier and contains more fats than any other. However, with the years the island's goats had become so degenerate that they were no bigger than fox terriers, and so Father Nicholas had written to California for two good specimens of the giant alpine breed. They had come, and now Diana and Jean are to improve the local stock and the priest is dreaming of the day when the islanders shall be bursting with health. Diana and Jean came with the post-boat. They were in kid when they arrived.

A five-year old boy seized me by the hand as I was walking up the village street and told me that I *must* come and see his garden. He took me to a little enclosure behind the school. It was carefully fenced in with plaited hurdles and there was a notice bidding all and sundry to remain outside, as the ground was the private property of eleven little boys. The garden had just been made. The beds were all sown and covered with twigs and seaweed, so that the birds should not eat the seeds. Charley and I were soon deep in a discussion of agricultural methods, I strongly upholding the advantages of crop rotation and importing *sajyha* potatoes. Then the teacher came out and invited me to go in and see the school.

The school consisted of one large room. Each corner was a classroom where the teacher and his three fifteen-year old assistants tried to make them-

selves heard and to interest their pupils in arithmetic, writing, bible history, geography, or whatever the subject was. Two of the youngest knew who Columbus was, but when I asked them what Denmark was nobody seemed to know what to say. Then they all lined up outside the school and in their clear childish voices sang a hymn to San Salvador. A hymn to that poverty-stricken, dreary, forgotten little island!

Of the islanders, the first he came across in the New World, Columbus wrote that they were " an inoffensive people, and so desirous to possess anything they saw with us, that they kept swimming off to the ships with whatever they could find, and readily bartered for any article we saw fit to give them in return . . . but they seemed on the whole to me, to be a very poor people." Heaven knows, that is true enough to-day, even though the population has been entirely changed since 1492.

Columbus was very nice to the natives. He did all he could to win them over and he issued the strictest orders to his people on the way they were to behave to them. However, his orders were not obeyed. When the Indians objected to their villages being plundered, the Spaniards dragged the male inhabitants away as slaves, and took their wives and daughters. The Whites took full advantage of their superiority in the arts of war and murdered them all in the course of the next few decades. Powder being expensive, the Spaniards as a measure of economy reared big dogs which were trained to tear the mutinous and peaceable Indians to pieces. Now, in several of the islands, there isn't a trace of Indian blood in the population, while of the aboriginees all that remains is one tiny colony of Caribs, the bellicose, cannibal inhabitants of the eastern Antilles.

The Indians were not good workers, and their place was gradually taken by negro slaves imported from Africa. It is their descendants who to-day form the bulk of the population on most of these islands which stretch in an almost unbroken chain from the Yucatan Peninsula on the east coast of Mexico to the north-eastern corner of South America.

For several centuries the coffee and sugar plant-ations on the islands flourished thanks to slave labour. Then slavery was abolished, yet on only one island, Haiti, did the negroes revolt and show their teeth so effectively that they were able to establish an indepen-dent negro republic in one half of the island. It still exists to-day, and the only difference between it and the other islands is that in Haiti the ruling class is black instead of white. There, as elsewhere, the great mass of the population still lives in the direst poverty, exploited, cowed, and apathetic.

With San Salvador Columbus did not discover the route to India, Japan and China of which he had dreamed. It was a malicious trick of fate to arrange that the first place in the New World on which he should set his foot should be one of the dreariest, flattest, least interesting of all the islands in the Antilles. It has never since its discovery been of any importance. For the English it is just a negative appendage to the more favoured islands in the

Bahamas, a yearly figure on the debit side of the budget.

Not even coconut palms grow on San Salvador. They flourish on the other islands which Columbus visited after this first landing. They are thick on Rum Cay; they wave in the Trades on Long Island and on Crooked Island; but on San Salvador they have died every time anyone has attempted to plant them. So even that addition to their diet is denied the poor wretches of San Salvador.

CHAPTER XVI

A Glimpse below the Surface

FERNANDA, despite the name, was no more feminine than a lusty six-foot negro in his prime ever is. Nor was Felix de Voux exactly what you would call a typical French aristocrat: he was thin, his hair was grey and he was always smiling; a sixty-year old negro, two of whose slave-ancestors had tried to flatter a popular French planter by taking his name. Fernanda was of Spanish extraction.

The two of them were perched on *Maria's* rail. Fernanda was smoking a thick cigar, while Felix thoughtfully picked his teeth. Fernanda was the head man of their team of two. He did the talking and consequently it was he who offered that they should come with us as bo'sun, act as pilots, supply us with sweet potatoes, teach us to fish, have their wives plait us straw hats of the local model—in that order. The last card they played in their attempt to raise a little capital was to offer to sell us for 25 cents a conch that Fernanda produced from the bosom of his shirt.

Fernanda was the aggressive type, so Felix had adopted a permanent exculpatory grin. Fernanda, in fact, was the only person on San Salvador with real initiative. He had once worked in the southern states of the U.S.A. and so his horizon was wider and his vocabulary larger than that of his fellow islanders.

He and Felix had just ended a lengthy discussion. It was a question of geography. Fernanda insisting that Denmark was a state in the U.S.A., Felix maintaining that it was to be found on the island of Cuba. It had been a fruitless discussion. Neither would listen to the other and we had given up trying to put them right as soon as we realized that their globe was a highly simplified one containing only two places, Cuba and the U.S.A., in which all others were located. Columbus had come from Spain, and Spain lay on Cuba.

It was a clear shining day. The swell had subsided and it was as much as the sea could do to muster a thin row of white teeth where it encountered the coral reef, which was gleaming with the colour of verdigris through the blue water. We had seen from the chart that there was a channel along which you could, if very careful, thread your way through the reef into the lagoon, where there was a tiny anchorage with two fathoms of water and a soft sandy bottom. I now told Fernanda to pilot us through.

This was our first coral island and I was dying to try out the diving tank that lay there in the stern. I had designed it myself, but it had been built for me by the best craftsmen to be had. It consisted of three parts, three round tanks of decreasing size that fitted one below the other, making the whole look like a half binocular. Four thick glass windows were let into the wall of the central compartment. The upper tank was open on top. The whole thing was supported by four buoyancy tanks bolted together. To submerge the three vertical tanks, they were provided with outside hooks on which we could hang over a half a ton of ballast which was made up in bricks weighing three stone apiece. The whole diving tank itself weighed almost as much as the ballast. The glass windows were so thick that no blow from a shark's tail could break them, and so large that the person within had a free view of the bottom on all four sides.

Niels and Jens were highly intrigued, but the skipper liked to speculate upon what would happen when we tried to lower the " contraption " overboard. He predicted first that, the wire would break; then that the boom would fall; that *Maria* would capsize, and finally that we would all drown if we escaped being eaten by sharks first. There was no greater optimist than our skipper.

We came through the channel in the reef with only two bumps; one on the pure white sand, and one on the wreck of an old steamer which had also tried the channel without our luck Having got there, we put out the tank. It only takes two seconds to write that, but to do it took a whole day. However, the wire, the boom, the boat, and the tank, stood up to it perfectly and the sharks never got a nibble at us that day. They were there, though; a row of them a little way out from the boat's side. That was because Niels and Jens were in the water, swimming about with a wrench in one hand, a hammer in the other, and a mouth full of nuts. They swam, and thumped, and cursed, and screwed, half the time with their heads under water so that we could not hear what they said, only see the bubbles of their words. In the end, late in the afternoon, there lay the tank, tied to *Maria's*

side, and it *floated*. Not only that, but it wasn't letting in so much as a drop of water. Jens and Niels were dog tired, but they had just caught a glimpse of the submarine panorama of the sea-floor and enthusiastically assured us that it had been well worth all their sweat and trouble.

We then rowed the tank into shallower water and it moored securely with an iron bar as anchor at a point where our water-glasses had shown the submarine landscape to be particularly colourful and diverse. After that, Fernanda piloted us safely back to the anchorage off Cockburn Town, for a narrow channel between coral rocks is not the best place to anchor in when the wind is liable to veer.

We were back again inside the reef by sunrise the next day. The tank was still there, pitching slightly in the morning breeze. We rowed alongside and clambered on to it. It hadn't shipped any water. Niels and Jens passed my cameras down to me as soon as I got in, and left me to my fate. Through the thick glass of my four windows I could see the " Caramel's " bottom as they drifted about with their own bottoms in the air and their water-glasses thrust below the surface, and I noticed how their excitement at times almost brought them to the point of capsizing. But I quickly forgot them and everything else except the scene around me.

At last I had reached a world that was really new, a fairy-tale world far more beautiful than any I had ever seen. As I watched, I forgot the disappointment of the dreariness of San Salvador, forgot time and place and all the difficulties with which we had had to contend. Here was I right in the palace of the Mermaid Queen, a world so beautiful and so wonderful that it surpassed even the most fantastic dream.

I was in the centre of a world of turquoise blue that stretched all around me for a distance of 25-30 yards. Beyond that, contours became smudged and colours merged into the deep ultramarine shadows that themselves melted into a deep-violet twilight. The floor of the sea was in places a golden brown, elsewhere turquoise blue. Out of this floor of dead coral and fine white sand the coral rocks rose up steeply, some like towers, others like ancient gnarled trees, others again like cacti or toadstools : it was a fairy forest, a landscape from another world, a Walt Disney fantasia.  Venus' fan grew everywhere, on the coral rocks, on the gnarled branches of those fairy trees, over the flat sea floor and the scattered small stones. Two to three feet high, in colour a delicate mauve, yellow or orange, it slowly swung and dipped in time with the passage of the waves above, or dropped in a curtsey with all the grace and charm of a ballerina.

I gazed and gazed and gazed. Every moment, some new feature would catch my eye. As the light shifted, or when a cloud passed across the sun, the strips of sunlight would race and gambol across the floor and all the colours would acquire new values. There were golden brain-corals, some tiny, some as large as millstones, carved in outlandish shapes just like the brain after which they are named. There were hard corals, covered with a layer of velvet, like that on a young roebuck's horns. And everywhere, all the colours of the spectrum. In niches in the rocks, on the sea floor itself, squeezing between the branches of the horn-corals, were black sea-urchins ceaselessly thrusting their restless six-inch spikes into space. Sea-anemones as colourful and variegated as orchids were opening and closing the dangerous cilia that fringe their greedy mouths. A squid scuttling backwards across an open patch of light blue sand left a billowing cloud of sepia smoke trailing behind it to veil its track. There were fish a yard long, fish no bigger than pieces of coloured confetti; blue fish and yellow fish, red fish and black fish, fish with stripes and fish with spots, colours so violently contrasted that it was difficult to believe these were living creatures and not bizarre  Chineses lanterns. There were large coal-black fish with a patch of brilliant yellow on their sides and long thin dorsal and ventral fins trailing behind them in the blue water; fish the length of match-sticks, of such a brilliant royal blue that they attracted your notice while still at a considerable distance. There, in the shadow of an overhanging piece of coral, was a massive, mighty giant fish quite motionless except for the continual munching motion of the great jaws that split it in two. It was like the witch lurking outside her hut to pounce on Hansel and Gretel.

The diving tank was lurching a little. At times its bottom would bump and grind against a coral block, or the side would ram a piece of horn-coral snapping some of its branches, and sending a cloud of golden particles spattering out from the break, and at once a swarm of small and large fish would rush in from every side and gobble them up.

None of the fish took any notice of the tank. They passed close by the thick glass window without noticing my face behind it, or stood in front of it moving their fins with lazy grace, before gliding slowly on. Even when Niels and Jens, abandoning their water-glasses, put on diving spectacles and plunged down into the coral jungle to cut themselves a Venus' fan from the ocean-bed, the fish refused to let themselves be disturbed. They might move aside to let  them pass, but otherwise they paid no attention to them.

Suddenly I saw a dark shadow appear in the distant background. Slowly it came towards the tank. As it drew nearer it took shape : I saw a slim body glinting with silver, a row of big shining scales along either side, like gleaming port-holes in the dark; tremendous jaws, half-opened to reveal a fearful row of needle-sharp teeth. At that, I roared up the funnel of the tank to Niels and Jens telling them to get back to the " Caramel " as quickly as they could, for we were receiving a visit from the tiger of the seas, the barracuda.

Unhurried and complacent in the knowledge of its invincibility, the barracuda glided through its realm. The small fish squeezed under the coral rocks and disappeared among the branches of the coral trees, for here was the devil himself come to their playground.

Native divers never have much respect for sharks. They will work quite unconcernedly in waters that are swarming with them. The shark is slow and a coward, the hyena and vulture of the seas; but the barracuda moves like lightning and goes straight to the point. It doesn't circle several times round an intended victim, leaving him time to think, as does the shark. It gives no chances. It hunts like the pike in our Northern lakes, and, indeed, its appearance is very like that of a giant pike. It can stand motionless under an overhanging cliff for a long time, waiting —and then it rushes like a thunderbolt at its victim and tears it open with its fearful teeth.

Calmly and quietly the barracuda went its rounds, rather like a policeman. It slid across my little coral realm and gradually disappeared again, melting into the deep blue shadow on the other side. However, Jens and Niels had lost their taste for diving that day.

The tank was now pitching so much that it was almost impossible to hold my cameras still. It swayed about like a drunken man, banging against the coral rocks on every side and making me bump my head against the glass of the windows and the iron rim surrounding them. Then the first water splashed in over the top and spattered down on top of me. More followed, and I had to crouch over the cameras to protect them from the salt water. The water began to rise in the bottom of the tank, but how could I even think of getting out when it meant tearing myself away from all that beauty?

The hours passed. The wind really was getting up and *Maria* was growing restless out there by the reef, for the wind had gone into the west, blowing straight on shore and rapidly whipping up a sea. Soon, I was standing in a continual shower-bath, and the tank resounded with its own rattling and booming. I now discovered a fault in my design: the round diving tank had four arms, one to each side, which rested on the rectangular buoyancy tanks. These arms should have been fastened down with a couple of bolts, but I never thought of its being necessary. Now that a swell had got up, the diving tank and buoyancy tanks rolled and pitched separately, each with its own rhythm, the diving tank bobbing up and down, the buoyancy tanks riding the swell. Each time the diving tank dropped, its four arms struck the buoyancy tanks with a rumbling noise, and drummed on the thin metal sheets of which they were made.

Clasping £400's worth of delicate photographic apparatus, I clambered up to inspect the situation. The seas were now splashing over the buoyancy tanks and pouring down into the funnel of the diving tank. The noise of the arms striking the tanks was bedlam. White foam had begun to appear on the waves out by the reef. The sun was very close to the western horizon. It was time to go.

Jens and Niels took my cameras from me. Fernanda and Felix tried to rope the four arms to the floats, but the angle irons had sharp edges and no rope would hold long. So, we rowed back to *Maria*, never taking our eyes off the diving tank, which danced and leaped twice as violently now that there was nobody inside. The waves were beginning to break against it and we could hear the hollow boom it gave each time the four arms struck the floats. Then the ropes parted, one after the other, and the diving tank soared right up to fall back again with a roar. Then, suddenly, one of the buoyancy tanks, tore itself loose and reared up

on its side in the water and so remained, towering over the others for an instant, pink in the glow of the setting sun. Then, it disappeared. The diving tank went down with a gulping sigh, and the remaining three floats drifted away across the lagoon.

We could see the diving tank shimmering whitely on the bottom. It had turned over and was lying on its side. Sixty yards away from it was a rusty boiler from a 5,000 ton steamer that had met its fate on the reef.

It was useless even to think of salvaging the tank, for it lay so far inshore that *Maria* could not get near it and there were no other means of raising it. To have tried to take *Maria* in would merely have been to lose our boat, and the reef round San Salvador had ships enough to its credit, judging by the melancholy legend of our chart, without adding to their number. And, anyway, our voyage was not yet over. Ahead of us still lay Rum Cay, Long Island, Crooked Island, all of which Columbus had visited on his impatient quest after China and Japan, and all the gold that he had promised to take home to Ferdinand and Isabella from the New World.

Poor Columbus! It would have been difficult for him to have discovered any poorer islands on this side of the Atlantic, than those of the Bahama group. To-day, they live on alms from London and off what they can beg from the stray tourists that come. Yet, though they had nothing worth exchanging, those poor Indians came out to Columbus with their small gifts before he sailed away. And so it was with us— or almost. When we went to the Commissioner to

Young Cuba

The anchor rattles down

say goodbye, the skipper and I were each wearing a brand new straw hat of local manufacture.

"Where did you get them?" asked the Commissioner, really interested.

"From Fernanda," said we.

"It was really nice of Fernanda to give you such a present!" said the Governor, smiling at the thought of his most forward subject being capable of such *grandezza*.

We said nothing. Out of us Fernanda had had as pilot's fee: a shirt, a pair of trousers, two cartons of cigarettes, three tins of meat, £1, a pair of old shoes and a smoked sausage; and even after that we had had great difficulty in pruning the price of the hats down from two to one dollar apiece.

And then there had been Felix. The moment we had finished with Fernanda, Felix came and began to tell us how much *he* wanted for sitting picking his teeth on the rail for three days on end, to say nothing of the valuable time he had devoted to sharing our three meals and our afternoon coffee.

"No," the priest had said the previous evening, "when these people see a strange ship approach, they don't think how pleasant it will be to have visitors to relieve the monotony, nor do they think of her lovely lines. Their minds are busy speculating over how much it will bring in if she runs on the reef; or, if she doesn't, how much they will be able to get out of the captain in pilot dues.

"Every service they do for a stranger has to be paid for. There is no charm about their begging, and you won't find them returning kindness with kindness."

F

They say that once, before the war, Winston Churchill visited Nassau. Then he went to New York. The reporters there asked him for his impressions of the Bahamas.

" A pirates' nest," said England's greatest statesman, who has always had a talent for hitting nails right on the head.

Now when we remember the Bahamas it is not of the flat dreary islands with their sulky black inhabitants that we like to think; but of our short and glorious venture below the surface of the sea, of our meeting with the marvels of that coral reef, and its whole world of fantastic, inconceivable beauty. Sometimes, I feel that that was a dream, yet the empty space in front of the deckhouse, where the tank used to lie, proves that it was real and that we had had to pay to view that unforgettable spectacle.

We sailed away from San Salvador with a course set for Rum Cay and Long Island.

CHAPTER XVII

The Priest who built a Church

FATHER CORNELIUS' straw hat was on the back of his head, and he had rolled the sleeves of his faded blue shirt up beyond the elbow, so that we could see the play of muscles in his strong hairy arms, of which no village blacksmith need have been ashamed. He was about to pull a tooth for the schoolmaster's wife, who sat there on a kitchen-chair, her mouth wide open and her tongue and gums looking *very* pink against her coal-black skin. Her eyeballs rolled as she looked apprehensively from the priest to us and back again.

"I shall be with you almost immediately," said Father Cornelius, taking a good grip of a molar with his forceps. Then he gave a twist of his wrist and a good tug, which brought his patient's behind off the chair. With a little gasp she tottered a couple of steps after him across the dipping floor.

"Damn!" said Cornelius, and thrusting his patient back on to the chair, he set his great left paw on her forehead, and pulled again.

A cry, a gasp, a tooth in the forceps and a dark red hole in all that pink; Father Cornelius flung the forceps on to the table on top of a copy of *Time*, wiped his hands on a blood-speckled dishcloth, and brushed the beads of sweat from his forehead. The schoolmaster's wife disappeared down the steps, holding one hand pressed to her face.

"Sit down," said Father Cornelius, clearing two chairs, one of a grey cat, the other of two plates and a dirty coffee-cup. "She was the sixth to-day, but I don't think there will be any more. If only I had a proper dentist's chair! You know, it requires a good deal of strength when you have to hold both patient and chair steady while you pull the tooth."

Somebody bellowed something outside, where two negroes had been very busy tinkering with an aged Ford when we came.

"O.K. I'm coming!? Cornelius shouted back, and, with a nod to us, disappeared down the steps.

Five minutes later he was back again.

"They never get the hang of it. God knows how many times I have shown them how to dismantle the carburretor and clean it ; but, nevertheless, every time it gets blocked, I still have to go down and help them."

He turned and looked out of the window. "It's no use doing that," he shouted. "You've got to swing it. The self-starter's dead."

A moment later there were a couple of loud explosions, followed by absolute silence. Cornelius disappeared again.

An old crone took advantage of his absence to creep up the steps. She stood there, holding on to the frame of the door and swaying like a drunken man. Then she stretched out a hand and asked for a penny. She was little more than a skeleton with black leathery skin drawn loosely over it. All her joints were swollen and rigid with rheumatism. Her legs were covered with scabby sores. She got her penny.

"God bless you. God be with you in all that you undertake from now on and till you die. The Lord's angels guard you, wherever you go . . . ." She went on and on in a monotonous voice, pouring out an endless blessing in a sort of mumbled incantation. Her eyes saw nothing. We sat there feeling both ashamed and moved : all that for a penny ! I wanted to smile, but no proper smile would come, for you can't relieve embarrassment just by smiling at a skeleton with a scabby skin, a walking corpse which blesses you for a penny.

Father Cornelius gave her a friendly clap on the shoulder, as he came up the steps again, and sent her away, still mumbling her blessing. It went on and on, as long as we could hear.

"She always comes to me," said Father Cornelius. "She has no one else to stick to. No one knows how old she is, but she's very sick—and very innocuous."

Into the priest's eyes had come a light, as warm and shining as that of a wax candle, and his hard Minnesota voice had suddenly acquired the tone of a child telling of a baby bird that had fallen out of its nest. And here, in that jumble of learned books and old newspapers, dirty cups, cigar-ends and bloody dish-cloths, I suddenly felt a waft of the true compassionate goodness and unselfish love of the Christian faith.

Father Cornelius is an American of German extraction. He once used to be a professional footballer and that is why there are several teeth missing in his upper jaw. He also has a squint collar-bone, due to a faulty join after being broken. I never saw him in vestments, but I don't believe they would suit him. According to him, he has a hard job living up to the legendary fame of his predecessor, Father Allan.

Father Allan is dead now, but he must have been rather a wonderful person. His first official act was to throw a police constable in full uniform out of a window without bothering to open it first. The constable had been pestering a nun. The local population chose to take that amiss and some of the negroes became impertinent. Father Allan knocked down any who did. After that, the negroes went on strike and refused to work for him. Father Allan was unmoved. Anyway, it was only the women, children and the old men who came to church. But he set all the young boys in the Catholic school to build a new garage for his aged car.

To-day, Father Allan's picture hangs side by side with that of the Virgin Mary in most of the huts and cabins in the island. Father Cornelius has replaced a man in whose footsteps it cannot, indeed, be easy to follow. But Father Cornelius is not only priest and pastor, friend of the lonely, and dentist; he also brought with him a complete set of surgical instruments for beginners. They are a bit rusty now, it is true, but then it is far from easy to set up inflammation under the cloudless skies of the Bahamas. So far he has successfully dealt with births, compound fractures, appendicitis, and one case of gangrene when he had to amputate a toe. He has no nurse to help him, and, of course, there is no hospital. He just washes his hands a couple of times in soap and water, and performs the operation on the dining-room table with the patient's family as his assistants.

He has been lucky all the six years since he first came to Long Island, but then, as he says, there are no germs in the air there. The islands are so remote that they haven't yet found their way there. Training? No, he never had any training. All his knowledge he has got out of the medical text-books that you can see lying cheek by jowl with religious writings and hand-books on mechanics in the rickety bookshelves.

His room is furnished with two chairs, a rocking-chair, a rickety table, a lithograph picture of Jesus, washing things, old boots, an alarm clock, two empty bottles of red wine, and the huge mail order catalogue of Sears-Roebuck, an organization that provides people in remote places with motor-car tyres, cotton aprons, screw-drivers, lawn-mowers, sweets, nylon stockings, flower and vegetable seed, and such like things.

Father Cornelius is also the island's only agricultural consultant. He it was who told me that Long Island was the place where Columbus first came across maize. It still grows there and is one of the most important items in the islander's wretched diet: a little maize, some groundnuts, a little sisal-hemp, and a lot of sour woody grapefruit; the whole lot of it poor and degenerate because of inbreeding and lack of manure. However, Long Island, and Rum Cay and Crooked Island, at least have coconuts, which San Salvador has not.

On Long Island, also, things have gone back considerably since the days of slavery. Here, too, the

planters packed their belongings and went away as soon as slavery was abolished. The blacks were left with an empty, brand-new freedom to starve to death. They had never learned to act on their own initiative, and now there was no one to tell them what to do to occupy their days; so, while they enjoyed their freedom, the plantations reverted to their original state, the cotton growing wild and the sugar-canes dying out. In the end, they were left with nothing but their freedom.

The Government has long since broken up the old plantation buildings and used the stones to wall in a churchyard, or to build a road.

" Just think," said Father Cornelius, " these lovely old gateways to the plantations, historical monuments, knocked down to fence in a churchyard! But it's almost all over now. It won't be long before the last relic of those days has disappeared. And no records have been made, least of all by the negroes. They are not interested in that sort of thing. They just sit with staring eyes and tell blood-curdling tales from the old superstitions of the Congo. They hand those on all right.

" They have no art, no literature—nothing. We have followed Columbus' track all round the islands here, and every time we have excavated in a bay which his Journal gives as having been inhabited by Indians, we have found fragments of richly ornamented pottery to bear him out, traces of a culture that the white man calmly and utterly destroyed in the course of less than a generation. And in its place came the negroes ! "

For all his multifarious duties Father Cornelius

has still found time to raise himself a monument that will shine out across the seas round the Bahamas long after the pictures of Father Allan have faded away. He has built a church on Gun Hill. Gun Hill is the highest point in the town, higher than the eminence on which the Anglicans built their white church thirty years ago. Gun Hill dominates the whole town, which is no doubt why a fort was once built on its top. Of that fort nothing but the name survives. Its cannons lie rusting on the sea-shore, to which, perhaps, the slaves trundled them down the hillside in the intoxication of their newly acquired freedom.

Two of these cannon Father Cornelius salvaged and planted in front of his church. He built that church himself, literally with his own bare hands that are hard and large like the paws of a bear. His congregation helped. They carried the blocks of coral-rag up to the site, mixed the mortar for him and handed him the stones, which he laid and fitted together, one after the other, until his white church stood ready. Now, it shines far out to sea, a wonderful shipping-mark for the few boats that stray into these parts. It has put the Anglican church quite in the shade, but that was only to be expected seeing that the same architect designed them both. He was an Anglican priest who, after making the drawings for the old church, later became converted to the Roman faith, and then drew the drawings for the new church which Father Cornelius built on Gun Hill. The two churches turn their backs on each other. The tower of the one faces the west ; that of the other, the east.

Father Cornelius' church has two slender towers

from which there is an entrancing view of the little
town, the green bay, and the deep, blue sea. It has a
cool and airy nave, and pointed windows whose frames
are of moulded cement. Each window is of different
design, copied from the leaded stained-glass windows
of older times. They had to be of cement to protect
the glass from the branches, tree-trunks, tiles and
sheets of corrugated iron that fly through the air when
a hurricane comes raging out of black clouds and
passes on its way of havoc through the Antilles in the
Spring. No hurricane can overturn Father Cornelius
church. He has used no timber, steel, or iron in its
construction. Mortar, coral blocks, and cement, those
were his materials ; that and God's help and the
strength of many willing hands.

Over the altar he has hung a home-made crucifix
It is childishly naïve, but pure, unconscious Gothic
It had been carved out of oak a year before and painted
in strong bright colours, a primitive piece of sculpture
to hang in a church so spacious that the effect is almost
barbaric. Then, in a niche in one wall, stands one of
the ordinary confectionery-work figures of the Virgin
Mary against a background of unhewn coral, just as it
was brought up from the tropic sea. The contrast
between the art of Nature and that of man is so crass
that you are inclined to believe it was a piece of
devilish irony. But that was not the intention. Father
Cornelius is not the one to scheme such things. However much one may inveigh against the polished
diplomacy and spider's-web organization of the Roman
Catholic Church, none can help feeling admiration
for the poor, hard-working, frugal-living priests like

170

Father Cornelius, who go out to the farthest corners of the earth to tell the heathens of the world that there is only one God.

CHAPTER XVIII

Cuban Landing

WHEN you have read Columbus' journal and a few hundred of the books that have been written about his voyages, there can be no doubt that he first went ashore on Cuba in the little bay that is now called Bahia Bariay. That was on 28th October.

What we ought to have done, of course, was to have landed in the same bay, but when we looked it up in the sailing directions we discovered that there was no town at Bahia Bariay, that it wasn't a port of entry, and that we risked a thumping fine if we went ashore on Columbus' deserted beach without first receiving the blessing and rubber stamps of the quarantine authorities, harbour police, immigration officials and customs officers.

A few miles from Bahia Bariay is a town of reasonable size, one of the most important on the north-eastern coast of Cuba. It, too, lies on a bay which received considerable mention in Columbus' journal, for it was the second place he visited and the one from which he sent his emissaries inland to seek contact with the country's king, the Great Khan, for he still believed that he had reached Asia and that the mainland lay just beyond these islands he had discovered. According to the sailing directions and the chart, there should have been three buoys at the entrance to

Puerto Gibara. When we reached it we found no buoys at all, so we sailed on in between the spots where they should have been, picking up a man who waved his arms at us from a tiny rowing boat. He, it appeared, was the pilot. The little boat was rowed by a man with a toothless grin, called Manuel. He ran his fingers through his hair and asked us for three cigarettes and to be taken on as seaman. To prove that he was in form, he clambered like a monkey up to the truck. Not having any use for a seaman—we were all officers on board—we took him on as handy man for the time we lay in harbour.

We asked about the three buoys. Manuel pointed to the head of the bay: there they lay in a row on the shore, just where they had drifted in twenty years before, only now they were red with rust and quite unserviceable.

Gibara is not the place it used to be. Before they built a road and railway across the middle of Cuba from east to west, Gibara was the most important shipping port for the whole of El Oriente, the name given to the north-east coast of Cuba which produces the sugar. In those days there were three large piers in the bay, and boats lying thick along each. To-day, all that remains are a few stumps of wooden posts that are now used only by the pelicans when in the evening they come flying home in regular formation and settle there for the night. Inland, the little village of straw-roofed huts to which Columbus sent his emissaries in the hope of finding the Great Khan, has grown up into a large town of 150,000 inhabitants and in doing so has throttled Gibara.

Hardly had our anchor dropped, before a motor-boat brought an engineer and a doctor alongside. They came aboard, and the moment they heard that we were following Columbus' route they grew so excited that they slapped our shoulders and told us not to worry about papers and all the nonsense with customs and police, that could wait till the morning or the day after, for this was a high holiday in Gibara. Also, as we were the first ship to have followed the exact route that Columbus took and had come to Gibara as our first point of call on Cuba, the doctor and engineer presumed that we agreed with what the people of Gibara had been asserting for centuries, that it was to Gibara Columbus had first gone and not to Bahia Bariay five miles further down the coast as certain inferior writers had sometimes alleged. I told them they were quite correct: it could only have been Gibara and nowhere else; and gave the skipper a warning kick under the table. It was an innocent little lie, for, as we discovered later, every town and village from Havana to Baracoa, claims categorically to be the point at which Columbus first landed. And the people of Gibara are so nice, that it would have been a shame to contradict them, to say nothing of the advantage of being fêted by a proper town instead of by the inhabitants of the two or three fishermen's huts, which is all you will find on the deserted shore of Bahia Bariay. As a result, we put on our gala uniforms and peaked caps and went ashore to join in the festivities.

Everywhere there are signs that Gibara was once a prosperous town. Just like a man who has lost so much weight that his clothes hang loose on him, so all the houses in Gibara are now too large. Many of them are shut up and empty. These were once the offices and dwellings of rich merchants. There are few taxis, and those there are, have not enough to do. Their drivers lounge at the street corners, and have long since given up soliciting fares, for they know that none of the passers-by have any need of a taxi, for this, the winter, is the dead period in Gibara. The summer brings American tourists and then the town comes to life.

In the winter Gibara is wholly Cuban, and the Cuban, like his island, is an individual, a personality, if there ever was one. Cuba was the last of the Spanish possessions in the Western hemisphere to free itself from the heavy yoke of Spain. That was in 1898. The story of that struggle is an epic that the Cubans never tire of re-telling. Although they threw off the Spanish yoke, the Cubans have not been able to free themselves of all links with their motherland, or rid themselves entirely of their heritage. Many of their habits are Spanish and familiar : clubs with their rows of arm-chairs in front of the entrance, the members playing dominoes, the dishes on the menu, the promenade on the plaza—they are all there. Then, the large, bare living-rooms surrounding a patio gay with flowers, the lack of any sense of homely comfort, the tre-mendous interest in politics, the fiery rhythm of the music—and over here it has more than a touch of negro tom-tom; these all show that Cuba is still not so very far from Spain. In certain ways, of course, you do notice the distance that lies between them. For

example, people are not nearly so afraid to remove their jacket and tie when it is hot; they have altered the Spaniard's lunatic timetable by which he dines at ten o'clock in the evening and goes to the theatre at midnight.

Gibara, being a town in retrogression, has the time to halt occasionally and draw breath. The tempo of life there is calm and dignified. Nobody in Gibara has restless hands or a nervously twitching face. Gibara, in fact, has accepted its lot. The morning after our arrival I went ashore. Within a short time I was stopped at a street corner by a man wearing a straw hat on the back of his head and a three days' growth of beard.

" Are you from the *Santa Maria*? " He asked.

" Si, señor," said I proudly.

" I'm from the Customs. Be so good as to come with me to the Inspector."

" Si, señor," said I again, feeling much smaller, for we had still not been cleared, and as we had spent all the previous evening and much of the night on shore, anybody of importance in the town was now smoking our " Admiral " cigarettes.

Gibara Customs office employs the nicest girls in the whole town, and the Inspector himself has a very wide embrace, which he needed to enfold me as he did. He first asked whether I was the new Columbus, who recognized that Columbus had first landed in Gibara. I told him that I was. At that he called me *amigo*, slapped me on the back, and stuck a huge Corona-Corona in my mouth, where I had to leave it for the next hour although I hate cigars. There were no reproaches for our having overlooked the prescribed Customs formalities, but, instead, a succession of baccardi cocktails and that brown beverage, *cuba libre*, which you know as rum and Coca-Cola. In fact, there wasn't a soul I met during our time in Gibara—not excepting the shoe-black on the pavement, who didn't slap me on the back and say, "Come and have a drink." It was the same with the skipper, and with Niels and Jens. The moment they showed themselves on shore : "Come and have a drink." Not that we objected, or at least only to Charlie. He had a Spanish name, but we found it easier to call him Charlie. He was a clerk in a grocer's and seemed determined to come with us by fair means or foul. The more cuba libres he drank, the more certain he became that his future lay on the high seas. In the end he went home and fetched all his papers and showed us that he had truthfully been born and vaccinated, and that he had never been in prison and was not liable to military service. Despite that, our hearts remained hard, for had we agreed to take him *Santa Maria* would have foundered under the weight of young men from Gibara who could see no future in their sleepy town and wanted to get away.

I returned from my visit to the Custom's Inspector late in the afternoon without having seen more of Cuba than broad smiles and empty glasses. I was dog tired and stumbled to my cabin and collapsed into a chair with a sigh of relief. Five minutes later, a motor-boat scraped against the side and a dozen doctors in white overalls poured on to the deck. Other people see elephants, thought I; but the doctors were real enough. The leader of the gang was my friend from

the day before, the quarantine doctor. He gave me four white tablets which picked me up in less than the five minutes I was given in which to change. That day, it appeared, was " Doctor's Day " and I was to be the guest of honour, firstly because I was Columbus, and, secondly, because I must be considered *Santa Maria's* doctor seeing that I had the key to her medicine chest.

" Doctor's Day " is an annual event in Cuba, similar in category to Mother's Day, Father's Day, etc. and Christmas Day. No doctor works on Doctor's Day. Any cases of serious illness are referred straight to the undertaker. When the doctors have finished receiving the presents sent to them by grateful patients, they put on their long white, short-sleeved overalls and go in company on a tour of the town's bars there to be honoured and treated. It was while they were in the middle of this tour that they had suddenly thought of me, and there they now were drinking gin in the saloon while I shaved as quickly as I could and tried to decide which tie was the least crumpled.

Going ashore, we found the town band swaying on its feet on the rickety jetty. It was an amateur band. The flautist was a waiter in the Hotel Campos. The horn was one of the town's leading baseball players, the guitarist an albino, and the violinist, as you could hear, really a pianist. The guitarist was playing with his eyes tight shut, (if he had opened them, he would have fallen down), the horn gave me a smacking wet kiss on the cheek, because, as he said, he loved Denmark. (He was a negro and did not seem to be quite sure whether Denmark was a drink or a new tune.) Then, we moved off. I in front between the guitarist and the black horn, behind me the flautist and violinist, and after them the doctors and a tail of inquisitive locals. We returned to the bar in which the idea of going to fetch me had first occurred to them. I was greeted by the owner; then one of the town's big businessmen came up, and he was followed by a string of others whose contours were so obscured in the clouds of cigar smoke that I could not make out who or what they were. All I know is that from their hands came an endless succession of glasses fragrant with brown rum. The Customs Inspector came and sat at our table and shortly afterwards disappeared beneath it. The band played " God Save the King " several times—in my honour!—then something that I was told was Toselli's " Serenade." That, however, luckily exhausted their repertoire of European cere-monial music and they then reverted to nature.

Rumba! Those who go to Havana usually visit the gramophone shops in search of the newest rumbas. Actually, those are the last places in which you are likely to be able to buy them. As a rule, new rumbas are highly Americanized products, made in the U.S.A., and the orchestration has nothing in common with Cuba except its use of *marracas*, those two calabash shells that, filled with gravel and fitted with a handle, make the rhythm regular and exciting. True rumbas, like the real popular tangoes in the Argentine, are old, old melodies, folk tunes that are used over and over again. While the American product arouses most enthusiasm in the dance restaurants of the rest of the world, few of them manage to penetrate into Cuba proper. Except in Havana, which is no longer Cuban but international and anyway destroyed by tourist hordes, the rumba is more sung than danced. In the villages, men and women meet outside of the four walls of their homes only on the few feast days. The woman's place is in the home, and the men can talk politics and play dominoes in the clubs and restaurants quite well without her assistance. That is another part of their inheritance from Spain.

At a quarter to seven in the evening, Gibara's mayor designate and president of the Doctor's Association, rose and declared the session closed. The festivities were over, and the members all got up to go home, have their dinner, and change in readiness for a further meeting in the Union Club, where they were to be guests of the Rotary Club. The orchestra wanted to come too, but the car-doors were slammed in their faces without mercy and the black horn, guitarist, violinist and flautist were left sitting sorrowfully on the coping of the pavement.

In the Rotary Club's big room stood a row of chairs facing the President's green table. The middle chair in the row was an armchair. That was where I had to sit. To the left of us was another row of chairs in which sat the members of the club, and on the right yet another for the doctors' wives. The president, vice-president, and secretary, took their seats at the green table, the bell was struck with a hammer, and the ceremonies began.

The first speaker reminded us of how that day had been chosen as Doctor's Day because it was the birthday of Dr. Findlay, the famous Cuban doctor who became one of mankind's greatest benefactors. He it was who discovered that yellow fever was spread by mosquitoes, and it was thanks to him that Gorgas was able to defeat the disease in Panama and that such pestilential spots as Santos and Havana became healthy ports and cities, to say nothing of all the other towns in South and Central America. When he had sat down, Dr. Washington Rossel stood up, pulled up his tie and replied. After four or five sentences of thanks, he said :

" We have in our midst to-day a Dane, who has just completed an exploit that brings us a message of Viking spirit and courage, a man with a mission . . ."

That gave me the shock of my life, and I blushed to the roots of my hair. He talked on and on, about Denmark's culture and love of peace, of H. P. Anderson and others, of the value of contact between peoples. I felt like a thoughtless schoolboy who has made a snowball with his hands on the top of a mountain, then dropped it, and sees it roll down and down till it becomes an avalanche and destroys whole villages. That wasn't what we had meant. We had set out just for the fun of it. Our country had not given us any mandate or duty to fulfil. I felt a cheat, an imposter who by false pretences had got hold of the incense meant for another. There was I stealing the limelight from those decent, hardworking doctors, merely because I had discovered the day before that Bahia Bariay was not a clearing port.

Then champagne was brought for us to drink the doctors' health, but instead they insisted on drinking mine, and so I had to get up and make a speech. There was a lump in my throat as I thanked them for their kindness and, then, to those friendly people I again made the vow that I had made to myself when I first began to write, that I would use my pen as a weapon in the struggle for international understanding, make it serve to help in breaking down the barriers that insufficient knowledge of others and antiquated prejudice have set up between races and nations. As long as any would read what I wrote, I would write so as to fight for tolerance, to combat chauvinism, narrow-mindedness, and all shams.

Thus it was that our arrival in Cuba ended on a higher, graver tone than that on which it had begun. I walked down to the rickety jetty and a gentle breeze drove me slowly out towards our little *Santa Maria.* A succession of falling stars kept plumbing the warm night. When I raised the oars out of the water, it was as though I had drawn them out of molten gold, such was the phosphorescence.

And such was our arrival at Cuba.

CHAPTER XIX

Fragrant Isle of Adventure

THREE rivers mouth into the bay at Gibara, which
Columbus called Rio de Mares. He thought that from
here he would be able to go overland to the city where
lived the king of the territories he had discovered, for
he felt that the mainland must be near, the rich East
Asia to which he persisted in believing he had found
the way.

Columbus tells that he found here lofty and beautiful mountains, *like the Peña de los ena morados, one of them
containing on its summit a protuberance in the form of a handsome mosque. The other river and harbour, where they now
remain, has upon the South-east two mountains of a round
shape, and at the West-North-West, a fine level cape
extends into the sea . . . This harbour which he called Puerto
de Mares, is, according to his account, one of the best in the
world, with a fine air and the inhabitants very gentle. Here
is a rocky promontory, upon which a fort might be built to
defend the port if this should become a place of any trade.*

You could not mistake it. That is an exact description of the profile of the coast at the entrance to
Puerto Gibara. To-day's *Sailing Directions* do not
express it nearly so clearly. Columbus then goes on
to describe how, farther to the West, was a cape
covered with palm trees. It is there all right, a low
long tongue of land striding out into the sea north-
west from Puerto Gibara, and it still bristles with

palms, arranged in rows like so may feather-dusters planted in sand.

It was here, at Gibara, that Columbus made one of his rare visits ashore. He seems to have been very loth to leave *Santa Maria*, but on this occasion he was richly rewarded. . . . *he rowed up the stream a couple of leagues to the fresh water, and going on shore, ascended a hill to take a view of the country, but nothing of the inhabitants was to be seen on account of the thickness of the woods, which diffused a very odoriferous scent, leading him to believe that aromatic plants abounded there. The beauty of the prospect was such that he declares his eyes were never tired of viewing it, nor was the harmony of the feathered tribe wanting.*

The two men whom Columbus had sent inland to find the town which he had understood the Indians to say was where the great king of those lands lived, returned from their mission with no news of the king. They had gone as far as where is now the busy expanding town of Holguin, and had found a pretty native village of some fifty houses and perhaps up to a thousand inhabitants, but no sign of the Great Khan or of the gold and other treasures of Cathay. What they did see for the first time was natives " with firebrands in their hands and herbs to smoke after their custom." Those herbs have proved of far greater importance to men and kings up and down the world than even the purest gold.

They came across other of the country's products spices that could be got from trees and bushes, yams or *potatos*, that they tasted there for the first time ; they found wild cotton and maize and beans, and lovely brown women who were by no means loth to be nice to these white men whom they thought had come from heaven. And the men stood by and nodded their approval, for the tribes of Northern Cuba had the same views on marital fidelity as the Greenlanders are said to have.

Columbus and his men stayed for eleven days in and around Puerto Gibara, and they seem to have made themselves quite at home.

*   *   *   *

The mayor's jeep drove on across the bridge. We had had to wait a bit to let pass a coach coming from the other direction. One vehicle at a time was enough. Enough! In Europe we would have said that one was too much, just as any European driver with the least respect for his car and his life would have pronounced the road on the far side of that bridge unsuitable for motor traffic. So, perhaps, it was; but nevertheless it was the main road to Santa Lucia and one of the best on the north-east coast.

Diomedes was driving. Jens and the mayor sat behind. The bridge consisted of loose planks laid over a framework of steel. It extended to within five yards of the far bank and there stopped. From where it ended, two planks, the distance of a car's wheels apart, led down into the water that at high tide flowed gaily between the end of the bridge and the river bank. The planks dipped under the jeep's weight as we drove down.

This was the river up which Columbus had rowed. The mangrove bushes extend all the way down it to the sea and in places wade out into the river on their tangled gnarled roots. Among these roots white herons fish. When you clap your hands, they rise gracefully and glide a little further into the mangrove bushes. From deep in among these bushes comes the deep cooing of wild pigeons, a virile, melodious and alluring sound, the signature tune of the Cuban woods, and high in the top of a tall tree sits Cuba's mocking-bird, the clown that imitates all the others, now the nightingale, now the doves, now the screech of a parrot.

The road followed the bay for the next three miles or so. It was high tide and the waves came sweeping and foaming right up to the road, so that one wheel was spluttering through water, whilst the other rode softly in the mud. We kept passing men on their way to town. All were on horseback. In a corner of their mouth they would have a fat cigar, on their head a flat Spanish hat or a broad-brimmed Stetson; round their neck a three-cornered scarf, and on their feet elegant boots with silver spurs on the heels. Their saddles were carved and inlaid with silver. Jens gasped, for he is a descendant of Doubting Thomas and had always maintained that such people did not exist except in films.

We drove through the country villages that were no more than two rows of wooden houses lining the dusty road, but in front of each house was a hitching-post and in the shops harness and lassoes hang from the ceiling among stable lanterns, barbed wire and bandages. Down one street a group of shouting men on horses came galloping towards us. The brown dust was wreathed and billowing behind them like smoke from a burning building, and the drumming of their small horses' hooves grew into thunder before they even reached us.

"It is a lie," said Jens. "But I know them well. I have often seen them in the cinema at home."

Beyond these villages stretches the primitive, untouched Cuba that tourists never see. Nor do tourists often see the places Columbus visited. The places that to-day are the great "attractions" in these tourist-ridden Caribbean Islands are all at some distance from the bays and river-mouths into which Columbus put on his way from San Salvador to San Domingo. These latter are still in a state of torpor, mere points on the periphery of the islands. They are untouched and still not threatened by any main road, railway or aerodrome ; their harbours are too exposed to the North-East Trades for the shipping companies to dare send their boats on a cruise of the West Indies along that route. So a ship or boat under a foreign flag is a rarity off Cockburn Town, Gibara, Mole Saint Nicholas, and all the other bays in which *Santa Maria*, *Pinta* and *Niña*, rode at anchor in the swell.

The mountains on the north-east coast of Cuba have been most carefully arranged. In other parts of the world, mountains are usually piled one on top of the other, or jumbled together, with the result that each steals the picture from the other. Cuba, however, has dealt with its natural beauties in a far more civilized fashion. Each mountain has been arranged separately, placed by itself on a tray, and draped in soft velvety folds. Consequently you can walk round it most comfortably, throw your head back or lay it on one

side and have plenty of time to enjoy its lines from every side and angle. Each mountain is a separate piece of sculpture, and each has its own characteristics. We had seen the mountains from the sea as we approached the coast, and now we were seeing them again from another angle. Columbus was indeed right to say of this scenery that its beauty was such that " his eyes never tired with viewing it."

There was the mountain he had described as having on its top a protuberance like a lovely mosque. There to the south-east were his two domed peaks : to-day they share the name of *Siella de Gibara* and are as distinct a landmark as those who approach Columbus' River of the Seas could wish to have.

How Columbus must have exulted when he saw the mountains of Cuba unveiled by the morning breeze ! Blue they must have been, just as blue as on the morning we saw them. What a relief it must have been to find such beauty and luxuriance after having strained his conscience to describe the flat dreary Bahamas in the enthusiastic terms necessary to save his face with the king and queen in whose name he travelled. In Cuba he had no need to call upon his imagination if his description of the island was to sound well, especially here on the north coast which combines the unobtrusive beauty of the plain with alpine majesty so harmoniously, that it could move even the most prosaic to write verse.

As the Trades drive across the billowing plain, they set hundreds of scattered palms gracefully waving against a background of slowing drifting cumulus clouds. The fields are fringed with hedges of agave, not the ordinary green sisal-agave that provides hemp for ropes and for straw hats, but purely decorative agaves of green and red that are only tolerated because their spiky thorns and tangle of thick-skinned leaves make a better fence than barbed or electrified wire. Behind these fences are the fields, stretches of rustling swaying maize or sugar canes, or great expanses covered with beans modestly crawling along the ground, for all that they are the main components of the islanders' fare and one of Cuba's most important exports. The most important, of course, is sugar which is the very corner-stone of the economy of north-east Cuba.

The peasants were busy among the half-withered bean-stalks cutting them and stacking them in great bundles, ready to be threshed. The threshing is done in the old primitive way which gave that word birth, with a flail. As we drove down the dusty road, we passed the huts in which these peasants lived. Their walls are made of palm bark with no windows and just a hole instead of a door; the roof is of palm leaves, the floor of hard-trodden earth. Hens, goats and small black pigs were scuttling in and out of the open door-holes, obviously just as much at home inside as were the naked brown children. Outside these huts, standing to watch us, there would as often as not be some adolescents dressed in old flour sacks that still bore the legend " Pillsbury's best " and a man with a huge cigar in his mouth. The woman of the establishment would be inside in the dusky gloom cooking a mess of roughly ground maize or beans over a smoking open fire.

These people seemed to be utterly poor, dwelling in the very nadir of life's exigencies, and yet the sun shines on their poverty and gilds it all the year round. And outside each hut, however wretched, flowers bloom in a riot of colour; bougainvillæa, hibiscus, frangipani, like fireworks against the blue sky with its silver clouds.

Down the road came a ragged man sauntering along with a sack on his back and a cigar in his mouth. Every now and again he would stop and sniff the mauve flowers that he held in his free hand. What a contrast there is between the flowerless, unimaginative poverty of the Bahamas and the smiling charm of Cuba!

We met little family groups wandering along in the dust. First came the children; then the wife carrying on her head a straw basket filled with bananas, oranges or washing; and the rear would be brought up by the man, on horseback of course, and with the inevitable fat cigar in his mouth, the horse pacing along sedately in step with the others.

In Cuba you will never see a man carrying anything except on a Saturday afternoon, when each and every one seems to have a cock clasped to his breast, bearing it as gently and carefully as a mother does her first-born. On Saturday afternoon and on most Sundays there are cock-fights in every village, in every large *hacienda*, and in every town, throughout the whole island. In the West Indies cock-fighting takes the place of bull fighting. From Trinidad to Yucatan, from Mexico right round the Spanish Main, each week-end sees cock-feathers flying across the sand of innumerable cockpits to the accompaniment of excited shouts.

The road was pitted with innumerable holes, but the jeep leaped them all like a frisky goat. It heeled over dangerously as we roared up the hills, and splashed through the shallow rivers in between. Twice it got stuck in the mud and had to be hauled out with a span of oxen. Such are the roads in Northern Cuba in the good season when no rain falls.

"A good thing we don't have to take the by-roads," said Diomedes, with an encouraging grin at Jens. We agreed.

Those who have learned to drive a car in Cuba have nothing more to learn. Diomedes juggled with the jeep's seven years as a virtuoso plays on the strings of a guitar, and it was not his fault that we twice had to have recourse to oxen. A jeep's motor is not meant to work under water.

The mayor's suit had been white when we left Gibara, but it was white no longer by the time we returned. However, we did see quite a lot of Cuba, and we also drove down to the silent shore of Bariay Bay which, you will remember, has wrongly been said to be the place at which Columbus first landed on this lovely island. It is an enchanting little bay. Mangroves and sea-grapes grow right down to the line of its chalk-white crescent of sand. A few wretched fishermen's huts stand hidden among the bushes, on which you can see an occasional wild cotton plant in flower, or a lobe-leaved ricinus with green berries like a candle round its stalk. (The ricinus is what provides castor oil).

As I stood on the shore breathing in the sea-air, it seemed to me that surely nothing had changed there since 1492. I would have found nothing strange in it if three caravels had suddenly appeared round the point and let their anchors drop with a rattle and splash into the clear water—but I was forgetting that it was in Gibara that happened!

The sugar-fields stretch down almost to Bariay Bay itself. We had driven for miles through green whispering woods of waving sugar-canes that were tall enough to hide a horse and its rider. In another two months the long *machetes* would begin to swing and Cuba harvest its most important crop. Santa Lucia, whose tall grey chimneys stand out like a navigation mark a little way inland, is the only sugar-factory in Cuba that is altogether in Cuban hands. All the others work on foreign capital, mainly American, for the U.S.A. dominates the industry and takes its entire production. However, it does not appear that the thirty-year old owner of Santa Lucia suffers greatly from their competition. His factory is a model establishment with pretty houses, each with a garden, for the workers, modern, airy schools for their children, hospitals, tennis-courts, football and basketball pitches, and a large and good restaurant, a park with a bandstand and swimming pool—all reserved for the workers and officials of the factory. Though Santa Lucia may be only an insignificant part of the Cuban sugar industry, it was certainly the finest and cleanest little community I had so far seen on the island.

Towards evening, when the sun was low down over Siella de Gibara, and the white herons were circling

Puerto Gibara is an old town

One of the old cannon from Gun Hill

slowly above the mangrove bushes before settling for the night, a shower of rain fell. It was only a short refreshing shower that soon passed, leaving the countryside clean and greenly shining; but with its going I sensed a new element in the air. As I breathed, my nostrils caught a balmy, exotic scent. It was sweet, yet without being cloying, and surprising in that though we were in the midst of nature's fresh greenery, I could have sworn that the scent came from a bottle. Diomedes noticed how I was sniffing.

"Yerba de ovejo," said he. "Sheep grass."

Then, suddenly, I noticed that the road was bordered with tall grass on thin silky stalks, and that this grass extended on and on to either side in great fields, in which brown animals were munching as they stood knee-deep. It bowed before every least puff of the evening breeze, and in the light of the lowering sun its colour shifted like the shot-silk of former days. It was from this grass that the heavenly smell came. As I shut my eyes for a moment and stood there, conscious only of that fragrance and of the soft warm air stroking my cheeks, I remembered Columbus' enthusiasm and sent him a grateful thought for having led us to Cuba.

CHAPTER XX

Cock-crow and Frenzy

ON Saturday afternoon, Dr Alberto, the children'
doctor, came up to me in the Union Club, stuck h
arm through mine, and asked me to act as his secon
the following morning I gazed at him in amazemen
Alberto is such a nice little man and certainly do
not look as though he went about insulting peopl
or taking their wives from them, or even telling th
truth about them. In fact, I should have said that h
was the last person in the world to have got involve
in a duel. However, he had done so much for me th;
I could not refuse when he came requesting a sligl
service in return; so I told him that I should be gla
to act for him. Nevertheless, it wasn't a cheerf
picture I could see with my mind's eye! I imagine
myself carrying his slender little corpse from the duellin
ground. Then I saw myself getting involved with th
authorities, with unpredictable results. (You mu:
remember that we had still not completed the entr
formalities.)

" What are the weapons? " I asked curiously. "
it's not yet decided, you plump for pistols. Sabr
make it such a protracted business."

Alberto looked at me, a puzzled expression in h
large dark eyes.

" Beak and claws, of course."

194

Then I understood. This was much more than being asked to second someone in an affair of honour. What Alberto was asking me to do, was to be *gallero* for his finest cock at the opening of the cock-fighting season the next morning. It is not easy to make you understand just how great an honour that was. It is roughly equivalent to being asked to look after the safes of the Bank of England while the head cashier takes a trip round the world.

"Alberto," said I, slipping off my stool at the bar. "Now I see that you really are my friend. Shall we open a vein and let our blood mingle, or shall I get Juan to mix us a rum and Coca-Cola?"

There are two galleros in the ring during every fight, each representing one of the cocks. Apart from the cocks themselves and the umpire, they are the only people allowed to remain in the arena. They are there to see that all goes as it should. Just as there are professional jockeys and gentlemen riders, so there are professional and amateur galleros. It sometimes happens that in the heat of the contest the two galleros come to blows. When that occurs the performance is suspended.

"I always like to study a thing properly, before I tackle it," said I to Alberto. "In the cold barbarian North, from which I come, we have few cock-fights and they are almost always confined to the poultry yard. Could you, perhaps, give me a short course in your national sport?"

Alberto agreed and we left the Union Club.

*   *   *   *

It was to all appearances a nice ordinary house in a nice part of the town ; but long before we reached it, we could hear piercing cock-crows coming from behind its tall fence and even from inside. It was, in fact, one of the best boarding-schools, training centres and clinics for fighting cocks. It had its own stud, but also accepted private cocks *en pension*. Altogether there were about a hundred cocks gathered under the roof and in the courtyard, each of them worth anything from ten to five hundred American dollars. A cock's value depends on its pedigree and on the qualities it has shown in earlier fights. Some are so valuable that there have been cases of one being swopped for an American car of the latest model. Altogether, the cocks in this boarding-house represented no small fortune, and they were treated like aristocrats. Each had its own private room. Their food was prepared by specialists with as much care as I imagine is taken in a royal kitchen, and certainly with greater knowledge of and more regard for such things as vitamins, calories and other ingredients likely to promote a fighting spirit. The actual formula used was a secret of the establishment, but it included such things as honey, corn, maize, bananas and minced meat. Each boarder's weight was constantly supervised, for a fighting cock must always weigh round about 2 lbs. 3 ozs.

Food and drink, however, are not sufficient to get a cock into its best form. It must also have sunshine and fresh air. So, every morning, the cocks are taken out into the yard and tethered by a short leash to a little stake. These stakes are sufficiently far apart for the cocks to be unable to get at each other with their claws and beaks, but still close enough for them to be a source of constant irritation to each other. If looks could kill, there would have been a hundred dead cocks lying on their backs in the sand with their feet in the air.

In one corner of the yard stands a sort of negro hut. Its floor is of the same size as that of the arena in the cock-pit and there is the same shadowy light under its straw-roof as in the arena itself. In this each cock is given a quarter of an hour's exercise every day. An assistant follows it round and round, driving it gently but insistently forwards with a palm leaf. It is never allowed to stop and rest, and if it takes to flight, it is very quickly forced down on to the ground again. Walk, run ; walk, run ; one, two, one, two . . . that trains the thigh muscles.

The cocks are of Spanish origin with a small admixture of English blood. They are trimmed in a very special way : that is, the feathers round the neck are clipped short, so that they look like a wig of bobbed hair ; the chest and underpart of the body are plucked, so that you could really roast any bird without further ado ; but the wing and tail feathers are left intact. Their colour is bronze in every shade and tone. There isn't a gramme of superfluous fat on any bird.

One wing of the house is equipped as a hospital. Like any ordinary hospital for humans, it smells of medicines and antiseptics ; and there are the same rows of bottles with vitamins, stimulants and dressings for wounds. After each Sunday during the season this wing is naturally pretty busy.

I was told everything about cocks and cock-fighting. I learned that the "noble sport" originated in India, China, and Persia in the days of yore, that the Greeks came across it during their campaigns in Persia and introduced it into Athens on their return. From there it spread to Rome and across Spain, France, the Netherlands and Germany, to England, and out to the Spanish Colonies, from which it was introduced into North America. It was prohibitied in many countries about the middle of the nineteenth century, for by that time it had assumed such proportions that there were cases of Irishmen and Englishmen holding cock-fights in churchyards, or inside the church itself. Now, Cuba is one of the sport's last strongholds, where cock-fighting still takes place openly and under Government control.

I learned, too, that the fighting cock of to-day is the nearest relation to the prototype of all cocks and hens, the Indian jungle cock which the zoologist calls *gallus gallus*.

Equipped with all this knowledge, I set out on Sunday morning for the arena in company with Dr. Alberto. Alberto was clasping a blue linen bag containing his most valuable cock, and I carried my cameras. We were quickly surrounded by a large crowd of admirers, for people now knew who I was; or thought they did. To some I was the man who had joined the doctors on Doctor's Day, a great foreign doctor, a sort of Findlay, Gorgas or Pasteur; while others had read in a special edition of the local paper devoted to our arrival how " Hakon Mielche proves that Gibara was Columbus' first landfall in Cuba." (Since Amundsen's discovery of the South Pole it had not used type of that size for mere geographical news.) I took some photographs as we went along, and each time I raised my camera, a shudder went through the crowd. At the entrance to the arena the crowd divided into capitalists and non-capitalists, and from then on all who wanted a further look at us had to buy a ticket.

People were streaming in through the door. This was the first fight after the three months interlude of the dead season, and everybody was there. The Mayor was there ; so was the Customs Inspector, and the Harbour Master. I nodded greetings to every side. Nothing but friends and acquaintances. Then the ceremony of weighing the cocks began.

The cocks were taken out of their bags and placed one by one on a perch mounted on a pair of ordinary domestic scales. The zealous eye of owner, controllers, opponents and umpire, watched the needle intently. It took a lot of fierce discussion before the weight was fixed to the quarter ounce and entered opposite the cock's name in the umpire's book.

People were beginning to take their places. The notabilities sat with their elbows on the rail round the arena. Behind them were the normal members of the middle-class ; and high up under the wooden roof sat the youths of the town and the really poor, those who could not stay away, but yet really could not afford to go. There were nothing but men, sweating men, apathetic in the heat that was already growing fierce under the roof, and all had a cigar firmly fixed in their mouth.

In one corner of the building was a bar. The whole place was gay with green, blue and red paint, so fresh that it came off on your clothes. This was the opening day of the new season.

The arena was some twenty feet in diameter and covered with a thick layer of sawdust, mahogany sawdust. In the middle was a large double cage made of wire netting over a wooden frame. One half was painted red, the other blue. The cage was fastened to a thin wire hanging from the centre of the roof, by which it could be quickly raised up out of the way; on top of the cage stood two basins with water and cotton wool, and also some sliced lemons to refresh the cocks between the rounds.

The people were all in their seats, and the first two cocks were having their spurs put on. A lot of care is taken to see that both cocks fight under equal conditions; they must weigh the same, and, if nature has given one longer or more pointed spurs than the other has, that is not allowed to affect the issue. The natural spurs are removed with a sharp knife, leaving only a stump that is carefully rounded. The cocks don't seem to mind this in the least, for they did not blink their eyes any more than usual. The stumps are then carefully washed with spirits, melted wax is poured over them and a pair of artificial spurs fitted on and fastened with silk ribbon which is also covered over with wax.

When it comes to the fitting on of the spurs, each owner produces from a pocket a silk-lined jeweller's

The cock-pit

On Cuba flowers bloom in a riot of colour

case—the poor are content with a matchbox—from which under the watchful eye of his opponent he extracts a pair of spurs one and three-quarter inches long. Each owner has his own ideas about the right type of spur. Some make them out of pigs' trotters, others out of tortoiseshell which is softened in boiling water, shaped and filed to a point. They can be bought in a shop for two or three dollars a pair, but the real specialist makes his own.

Each measures and inspects the other's spurs, protests and appeals to the umpire. It seems as difficult to choose the right spurs as it is for a woman to select a new hat. Eventually, however, agreement is reached, and the two cocks have had their spurs fastened on securely and have been carefully placed in their part of the cage in the arena. Then the umpire shouts, "Everybody out!", and they go, leaving only him and the two galleros in the arena.

Dr. Alberto's cock was the first to fight. I now found myself alone in the arena with the umpire and a gigantic negro. I had put Alberto's cock in its cage, stroked its feathers, and whispered something to it in Danish. Then, as instructed by Alberto, I stood by the side of the cage and banged on the wire to cheer the cock up, swore at it to make it angry, and praised it when it flapped its wings, or kicked at the wires when it seemed to be sunk in its own thoughts.

Then the umpire took a little hourglass from his trousers' pocket. It was just an ordinary egg-timer, but it plays a great part in the fighting. The spectators now began to bet. They looked at the two cocks and carefully ventured a shilling on one or the other. I put two bob on my cock. My opposite number, the negro, flung a dollar on the cage and looked derisively at me. I gave the cage an extra kick and Sandy gave a start. I called him Sandy, because I have a friend of that name who is just as red in the comb.

"Get to your places!" cried the umpire. The negro and I rushed to the fence round the ring and squatted down. The cage was jerked up into the air, and the two cocks flew straight at each other. The first bout of the year had begun.

I kept hens during the war. I have often seen cocks fighting in a poultry run, and I must say that I found this fight at Puerto Gibara no whit more exciting than those domestic bouts. They flung themselves at each other's head, and a few feathers flew. Then they did the same. After that they walked about for a bit on stilted legs glaring at each other, and then they flew at each other again. That was all.

But the spectators! I forgot all about my duties as second in looking at the spectators. Those who, a few minutes before, had been hanging indolently even apathetically, over the balustrade, were now transformed. They leaped to their feet, flung their arms about, pointed at each other—and yelled. At first, I thought they were screaming threats at each other, that the commotion was a sort of prelude to mass murder, but then I made out some of the words

"*Uno para cinco!*"
"*Uno para diez!!*"

They were calling the odds: five to one in pesos Ten to one. Each peck made the odds rise. First one cock, then the other, was favoured. The odds soared and dropped again, like the curve of a seismograph. Ten pesos, twenty, fifty—a hundred, screeched the mayor, puce in the face, brandishing his index fingers like a runaway metronome. A hundred pesos is £35, for the peso is equivalent to a dollar. Now I understood how people could exchange a 1948 Buick for a cock weighing 2 lbs. 3 ozs.

Meanwhile the cocks were flying at each other incessantly. Then, suddenly, my counterpart, the opposing cock's second, lost control of himself. He stood up, one arm flaying the air, the other hand tugging at his one trouser leg until it was above his knee; then he began dancing about on bent knees, his wide-open eyes rolling in his black face. Then he seized his hat, threw it to the ground and trampled it, foaming at the mouth and bawling. The people at the balustrade, unable to see for his tall swaying body started shouting, " Sit down ! " He gave a start and squatted back on his hunkers, his right hand still clutching his trouser leg, his fingers clawing ceaselessly at his knee. He did not know that he had ever stood up. That is ecstasy.

The feathers were flying. Then, suddenly, our opponent's cock could fight no more. It lay down on its back in the sawdust, and Sandy got up on it and looked proudly around. The umpire turned his egg-timer upside down and gazed down at the red trickle of sand. When this stopped he would separate the two cocks, set them on their feet, breast to breast, and see what would happen.

The cock would fight no more. Sandy seized it by the comb. My negro gave a bawl. Then the two cocks

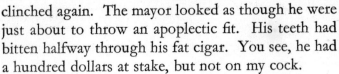

clinched again. The mayor looked as though he were just about to throw an apoplectic fit. His teeth had bitten halfway through his fat cigar. You see, he had a hundred dollars at stake, but not on my cock.

Again the cocks were separated and set breast to breast, but the other had now had more than enough. It took to its wings and flew out over the balustrade, straight at the head of the poor mayor. Jubilant cries greeted its flight. The negro dragged his trouser leg halfway up his thigh, while his free hand tore at the short tufts of wool on his head.

Sandy, meanwhile, stalked stiffly about the arena. Then the umpire raised both arms above his head and Alberto leaped over the balustrade, caught his cock, clutched it to him, and kissed first it and then me. The fight was over. I picked up the negro's five dollars and left the arena.

As we stood at the bar, the owner of one of the next cocks came up and asked if I would not second his bird. Hard on his heels came the owner of the other cock with the same request. Evidently, I brought luck, was a sort of amulet. Looking round, I saw the owner of the cock Sandy had defeated standing in a corner weeping tears of shame. I excused myself from any further seconding, saying that I had to be getting on. And so I had, for we had to go on to Haiti.

We sailed the next morning as the sun rose, as red in the comb as a prize cock.

CHAPTER XXI

The Pirates' Hunting Ground

WHEN he left Gibara, Columbus was still clinging to the theory that the new world he had discovered was really the mainland of Asia. He was in daily expectation of reaching the realm of the Great Khan and sent emissaries inland to follow up every tip the kindly natives gave him. When they returned, it was always without news of the mighty chieftain they had been sent to find, and all that they had to tell was of the small villages they had seen.

Columbus was searching for gold, the gold he ought to, had to find, to placate the rulers of Spain who had equipped his expedition. Impatiently he searched for his "Great Khan" and his gold all along the north coast of Cuba. And he sailed eastwards *against* the wind, the North-east Trades that blow with almost constant steadiness along the shores of Haiti and Cuba. And always he made meticulous notes, so that his journal with its exact descriptions of the bays and river mouths, the promontories and mountains, that he passed as he sailed along, is as good as any book of sailing directions. He was the conscientious seaman who thought of those who would follow in his wake. He noted down his suggestions for places where towns and forts might be built in the future, and the future approved them . He was also something of a botanist and zoologist, for he describes in some detail the plants and fruits he found. He investigated the soil and discusses which of the European semi-tropical fruits it might be possible to cultivate in the islands to the greater profit of Spain. The general impression you get from reading his journal is that he must have been an engaging character, and certainly an unusual one in those days, when everybody, from the king at home to the youngest ship's boy on board, was consumed with a thirst for gold, pearls and other easily earned riches.

Columbus had an eye for the future and for development, the true eye of the colonizer—at any rate in theory. And he was wise and sober-minded in his treatment of the natives. Again and again his journal stresses that they were to be treated humanely and not to be frightened, and time after time he had to punish members of his crew who disregarded these orders. Had Columbus been allowed a free hand, it is quite possible that the conscience of the white race would not be pricked, as it is to-day, when there is talk of its colonization of the world Columbus gave us. But, idealist and dreamer that he was, Columbus was shoved aside by men athirst for gold, with the result that the Indians of the Caribbean were slaughtered and exterminated before Columbus had been dead a hundred years.

Dreamer and lover of beauty—an unusual type of man for those days. You grow to like him as you read, especially from those unforgettable passages where in his slight seaman's vocabulary he makes fumbling attempts to express his joy in nature, always making comparisons between the islands and his beloved

Andalusia : " Everything looked as green as in April in Andalusia." " The nights mild like May in Andalusia." Always Andalusia. How those rough conquistadores must have laughed at him with great slapping of thighs, at that man into whose eyes tears would come when he heard a bird sing, and he an admiral ! But I bet none dared grin or laugh at him openly ! They might, perhaps, have done so before the three boats sighted San Salvador, when there had been that threat of mutiny, but once Columbus had proved that he was able to lead them across the wastes of ocean to the New World, there was no further hint of insubordination, for who else but he would be able to guide them back again to Spain ? If there was an exception, it was Columbus' second-in-command, Martin Pinzon. He seems to have been difficult and often obstreperous, presumably out of jealousy. Although envious of his chief's success, he had at least had the comfort that Columbus had so far failed to find the gold that he would have to produce, if he were to remain in favour after his return. It was the gold that mattered, so, after leaving Puerto Gibara, Pinzon set off eastwards in the *Pinta* on a little voyage of discovery of his own to the fabulous island of Babeque, the present-day Great Inagua, most southerly of the Bahama Islands. Some natives had tipped the island as a likely place in which gold might be found, and Pinzon hoped that he would be able to get in first. This tip, however, proved no more reliable than those Columbus was always receiving, and Pinzon was disappointed.

How little things change! The Spaniards asked the natives of those days for gold, and were assured that it was to be got in great quantities. Now, although the islanders are of a different race, they are really just as primitive and just as loath to disappoint a stranger, and so if, when asking the way, you say to one, "It can't be so very far to Tanamo?" the answer will always be a friendly "No, indeed, not far at all." But, should you say, "Tanamo is a good distance from here, isn't it?" the negro will nod his head in eager agreement and answer, "Yes, it's a long, long way away." In other words: always agree with a stranger. Primitive people all the world over hate to give a negative answer.

Pinzon returned from his little voyage of discovery with empty hands and—if I may be allowed to mix my metaphors—with his tail between his legs. He had disobeyed orders and he came back cringing, but Columbus did not take it out of him. Others would have strung him up at the yard-arm for mutiny, but Pinzon got off scotfree. And now there is a marble statue to him in the market-place of his home town.

As he slowly made his way along the north-eastern coast of Cuba, Columbus put into several small bays and sailed up various rivers, collecting samples of spices and fruits, making comprehensive notes and taking aboard Indians whom he intended to train as interpreters. It was arduous work backing up against the stiff Trades, and on occasion Columbus had to seek shelter. Once he found it in the well-protected Tanamo Bay where the floor of the anchorage is fine and soft, and the country green and lovely; and again in Puerto Cayo Mao, where he sailed up the river and made careful notes ranging from bird-song to the presence of trees tall and slender enough to make masts for the largest ships of Spain. He suggested this as a good place for a future shipbuilding yard— he was always on the look-out for places that would be useful in colonization—and there to-day there are sawmills, large and small, busy sawing up those trees from the forests of northern Cuba : tall slender firs, the *pinus cubensis*, and the famous Cuban mahogany that has that lovely fine braiding of leaves.

Columbus sailed on and on, noting nine excellent harbours, but without going into them, and all the time he passed the loveliest imaginable mountains and glens, small islands and wooded promontories. And all the time the weather was against him, the wind contrary. Then one day it abated, and Columbus decided to stand out from Bahia Baracoa and continue eastwards. And there, to the east of the headland he called Cape Alpha and Omega, now Cape Maisi, he made out on the horizon the dim outline of a large new island : Haiti.

His little fleet of two boats steered across the Windward Passage, so frequented by shipping to-day, onwards to fresh adventures.

It is only a short passage, not much more than fifty sea-miles of open water, but the sea was choppy, the Trades blowing hard, and the current carried us to the south. *Maria* settled on her side with the whole rail under water and leaped about like a colt in the first days of Spring. We took in sail and she righted herself, but then the wind freshened and she heeled over again. She was not a pleasant boat to be in then; no boat is when you have reached the state of wondering whether it would be easier to go by the lee stern or by the after-peak, as we did, for we had lain too long off shore in Cuba and the Bahamas, so that we had become soft and were having difficulty in finding our sea-legs again.

At sunrise we had had Cape Maisi abeam. It was not till the sun went down astern that we ran into the lee of Cape Saint Nicholas and put into the ideal little harbour there, which had also received the first *Santa Maria* on 6th December, 1492, St. Nicholas' day. We let the anchor go among the reflection of the tall green mountains that mirror themselves in the waters of the bay, mountains more savage and compact than those of Cuba.

Haiti Columbus called *La Isla Española*, but later people went back to the original Indian name. Port Saint Nicholas, is still called Port Saint Nicholas, but Columbus' prophecy that this safe harbour would one day develop into a place of prime importance, has not been fulfilled. There is nothing there but an insignificant little village mainly inhabited by fisher folk, and its roads are only used as an emergency anchorage by ships that have found the Trades too strong for them, as we had, and dare not risk attempting the Tortuga Channel, that short stretch of ill-repute between the north-west coast of Haiti and the little island of Tortuga, famous base of the pirates.

The age of the pirates lies midway in time between the voyages of the two *Santa Marias*. It begins in the colourful seventeenth century, when those bloodthirsty men with the more or less official support of their governments at home first began worrying at the hitherto all-powerful might of Spain. There were Englishmen, Dutchmen and Frenchmen among them. Some were bloodthirsty, brutal butchers and bestial sadists, others capable, resourceful men of the Robin Hood type, but they all had the same object : to loot as many as they could of the transports that carried the wealth of the West Indies and of South and Central America across the Caribbean and home to Spain.

The islands of the West Indies made ideal hide-outs for people with initiative and piratical intentions. They contain endless little bays that are screened from the sea and only to be approached through highly dangerous coral reefs that only those with local knowledge can navigate safely. Throughout the previous century Spain had regarded the Caribbean as its own private lake ; but as the Conquistadores who had followed Columbus made their way across to the mainland of South and Central America to the gold of the Incas and the wealth of Mexico, the adventurers and adventurous of the other European countries had poured in and settled on such islands as the Spaniards had never bothered about.

To begin with it was merely a case of the other nations subsisting on the crumbs that fell from the Spanish table, but gradually little colonies and trading companies grew up on the islands. Their connection with their home countries was of the slightest, but they made excellent accomplices for the pirates whose schooners flitted in and out of their bays and harbours, bringing above all money to the islands.

There isn't an island in the Caribbean that hasn't an exciting history of its own and its tales of buried treasure. To bear them out, sometimes a golden Spanish doubloon or two is found gleaming on the shore after a storm. The pirates seem to have buried their treasure, as dogs bury bones, and every now and then a hempen rope would prevent the owner coming back to dig it up again.

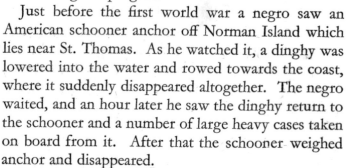

Just before the first world war a negro saw an American schooner anchor off Norman Island which lies near St. Thomas. As he watched it, a dinghy was lowered into the water and rowed towards the coast, where it suddenly disappeared altogether. The negro waited, and an hour later he saw the dinghy return to the schooner and a number of large heavy cases taken on board from it. After that the schooner weighed anchor and disappeared.

Then the negro himself rowed across to Norman Island. He found a low entrance to a grotto in the cliff and rowed in. Peering into the water, he saw something glinting on the bottom and diving down, came up again with a Peruvian doubloon minted in Lima in 1739. It was then worth twenty dollars. Nobody has ever discovered who owned the schooner, or where she went. Now, there are only bats in the grotto.

These tales of buried treasure are always popping up, now here, now there. Many are born in people's imagination and day-dreams, others are true ; but as long as the spirit of adventure still dwells in man, there will always be secret expeditions fitted out and mysterious ships that set course for the maze of islands of the West Indies.

The treasure, however, was not all buried. Some was lost in regular sea-fights with enemy ships, or in cyclones. For example, in 1637 sixteen Spanish caravels went down somewhere among the dangerous Bahamas. One was raised in 1687 and proved to contain gold that now would be worth two million dollars. The other fifteen are still there. Three tons of gold were lost in *The Golden Pig* that went down to the south of Haiti. That was in 1796, and no one has yet recovered it. In 1812 the frigate *Don Carlos III* disappeared with a cargo of gold worth a million dollars. Those are but a few of the enticements the Caribbean still has to offer those who, like the pirates of old, prefer to get rich quickly or go down in the attempt.

On Martinique, St. Kitts, Barbados, Tortuga, St. Thomas, no matter where, a pirate schooner was always welcome, especially after a successful coup. When the motley crew went ashore, they spent their money open-handedly; wine appeared on the table and music played. The pirate skipper would do his business with merchants who never worried much about the origin of the goods they were buying, as long as the quality was good and the price right. The city fathers and harbour authorities winked their eyes when ships came in to repair damage suffered in a sea fight, with sails to be sewn and men to patch, and provisions to be bought for the next expedition. Many a West Indian business, to-day of unimpeachable repute and highest esteem, was born of this trade.

It was no easy route that from Panama, the nodal point of the Spanish gold transports, to the harbours of Southern Spain. The two main strongholds of the pirates were Jamaica and Tortuga. Tortuga—there it was on the farther side of a little sound no more than five miles across. There is nothing striking or dramatic about its appearance. It is inhabited by poor decent negroes who cultivate a little land, catch a few fish, and beg a dollar or a cigarette from any tourist who happens to stray their way. Yet, there was a time when Tortuga was stiff with gold, when it was such a haunt of the pirates that people, believing the old saying that bird's don't foul their own nests, never even thought of locking their doors at night. And from Tortuga death and destruction went in search of the Spanish fleets.

Can you recall the name of Pierre le Grand? He was a Frenchman. One day he packed twenty-eight men into a boat that could scarcely hold them, and with it crept up alongside the Spanish Vice-Admiral's ship that, conscious of its own superior power and heavy cannon, was sailing alone through the Windward Passage without any form of convoy. The Admiral and his officers were playing cards in the wardroom, when Pierre le Grand and his twenty-eight men clambered over the rail, after sinking their own little craft and with it any craven thought of retreat. They took the ship with just their pistols and knives, and the booty was so enormous that they were all able to retire and live as respectable citizens for the rest of their lives.

Do you remember Henry Morgan, who came of a good Welsh family and was shanghaied and taken aboard a boat bound for Barbados? He served his time on her, and then he set up on his own and did business under the skull and crossbones with a success that few others have ever had. He it was who assembled 2,000 men and 39 ships at Tortuga, sailed to the isthmus of Panama, overwhelmed the fort on the east coast, and marched through the jungle at the point where later the Panama canal was cut, and fell upon the enemy in his own capital, the city of Panama, on the Pacific.

He took it after a twelve-hour fight and returned with fabulous loot. Later, he moved to Jamaica, where he became good friends with the Governor. Then, several years later, he made the voyage back to England where he was knighted. Then he was sent back to Jamaica as its Governor, and, as such, he waged fierce warfare against piracy in the Caribbean.

The age of piracy in those waters was almost over. The Spaniards had gradually come to feel themselves so weak that they preferred to send their precious cargoes from South and Central America the long and dangerous way round Cape Horn. There was nothing in piracy any more, and the great ones left the game. In the end, there were only the smart business people left, whose descendants still plunder the unwitting tourists who go ashore from the big American tourists ships that cruise in the Caribbean.

The clink of gold earrings and heavy golden chains still echoes in the names of many of the little islands, bays and reefs: Rum Cay, Flanagan's Pass, Blackbeard's Castle, Bloody Bay, Dead Man's Chest—

"Fifteen men on a dead man's chest,
  Yo-ho-ho and a bottle of rum!
Drink and the devil has done for the rest—
  Yo-ho-ho and a bottle of rum!"

If you listen hard, you can still hear a faint ring of ducats and hoarse cries borne on the Trades from Mole Saint Nicholas. But it is only ghosts that are left. Tortuga has relapsed into poverty and been forgotten, so let us take up the thread of Columbus' voyage again and sail on along the north coast of that curious country, Haiti, where Columbus at last found the gold he had to have, and where he lost his ship *Santa Maria* on Christmas Eve, 1492, and from her wreckage built the first fort in the New World.

Washing in the river : an African idyll in Haiti

Irrigation is essential for growing bananas

CHAPTER XXII

A Study in Black and Red

COLUMBUS may have been a superb navigator, but as a journalist he was a tiro and made the mistake of most beginners when they first come to an exotic country : he used up all his best and most picturesque adjectives right at the start, only to find a few days later that there were places still more *beautiful*, still more *enchanting*, still more *paradisical*. Columbus admits it in his journal, confesses it in his letters to the king and queen, when he begs them to believe that he was not exaggerating when he told them in previous letters that he had found the world's best harbour, the world's most beautiful river, and the nicest natives in the world. He had; but unfortunately he had kept on finding even better harbours, rivers still more beautiful, and natives who were nicer even than the last ones he had encountered. He used most of his adjectives on the Bahamas, and in his enthusiasm over the beauties of Cuba, exhausted the rest of his vocabulary there. Then he came to Haiti and realized that he should have kept most of them to describe it.

It was on Haiti that Columbus for the first time met a real native king, a *cacique*. He was a young man of about twenty and still as naked as when he was born. For all the lack of gold and ermine, however, his bearing was so dignified and he was so obviously a ruler, that Columbus was impressed. From Columbus'

description of him and of his people it seems fairly clear that the natives of Haiti were very far from being " savages." They behaved with calm *grandezza,* treated the whites with the greatest courtesy and helpfulness, with never a thought other than that they should behave with the utmost consideration to this handful of men who had come to them out of the blue horizon in ships the like of which they had never seen.

The thought occurs to me of how the cultured natives of England, Spain, France, or the U.S.A., would behave in similar circumstances. If such a strange ship with a similarly strange crew were to arrive and anchor off one of those coasts, what sort of a reception would the newcomers be given?

Once the immigration officers, quarantine inspectors, customs officials, and other members of the staff of our modern Inquisition, had finished with them —which would not be for a long time—the reporters and press photographers would be loosed in upon them, and I bet that before long the poor wretches would have fled back to their ship in an attempt to escape the flood of questions and the bombardment of flash-bulbs with which our " civilization " would have overwhelmed them. Or, if they dared to go ashore, the police would have to turn out in force to defend them from young girls wanting to kiss and be kissed, and young boys wanting autographs and cigarettes.

That is how we would treat them; but Columbus and his men were overwhelmed with gifts ranging from heavy plates of hammered gold to foodstuffs and tame birds. The *cacique* gave orders that all members of the crew who came ashore were to be entertained and treated with the greatest possible courtesy. To quote from Columbus' *Journal* for Thursday, 13th December, 1492 :

> *The Indian who accompanied the Spaniards under-standing that the Admiral wished to obtain a parrot, told this, as they were led to suppose, to the inhabitants, who brought great numbers of them immediately to their guests, and gave them as many as they desired, without demanding anything in return.*

And from *my* diary for 13th December, 1948 :

Niels put me ashore. No sooner had I passed through the gate than five or six buck negroes crowded round asking me whether I wouldn't like to see some white girls dancing the rumba, or to buy a genuine voodoo drum, or some unusual postcards ; or, finally, wouldn't I like to hire a taxi very cheap, only eight dollars an hour. I walked quickly ahead, my eyes fixed in front of me, but they clutched hold of my sleeves and continued to pester me with further suggestions.

In the end, I stopped, turned round and made them a little speech. I explained that I was not an American, not even a tourist ; that I had no money, and that I was on my way to the Danish Consulate. Their answer was to offer to show me the way to the Danish Consulate. I shook my head and walked on faster than ever, for I know that negroes do not approve of doing anything quickly in a temperature of 95°F. Two of them stuck it out and we reached the consulate almost simultaneously, However, only one had the cheek to follow me in and demand a dollar for guiding me there from the harbour. The consul soon disposed of him.

The same thing happened to Jens, when he went ashore later in the day. Jens, however, does not speak French ; and when he gets annoyed, he looks very fierce and there is a threatening rumble to his voice. He was followed up and along the main street, and in the end the negroes began throwing stones at him. Jens went back on board at once and swore that never again would he set foot on that damned " nigger land."

Wherever you go, women, children and elderly men appear, pluck you by the sleeve, and say: " Give monne ! Give monne ! " which is by no means a request, but a demand. You have only to stop a moment in front of a shop's window for a shoal of little boys to gather round you, offering to show you this or that. One and all have an impudent glint in their eyes, and if you refuse to speak with them, they immediately become downright offensive. They are a pest.

Because they are such a pest, my first task must be to try to find the reason for the radical change in conditions that has come about since Columbus landed in Haiti and was met by natives who gave with both hands without asking for anything in return. This means delving a little way into the history of Haiti, which is as dramatic as any film, colourful and simply dripping with blood.

The Indians Columbus came across on his first voyage were gentle hospitable farmers and fisherfolk who, though perhaps on occasion they might have had a bone to pick with a neighbouring tribe, seemed to have been normally peaceable and peace-loving. The farther east he went, the more obvious it became that the brown-skinned people of the islands were afraid. Fear was in their blood. They were not nearly so confident in coming down to the shore, as the Indians in the Bahamas had been. In many places they fled into the woods whenever they saw Columbus'

ships come into the bay. It was the Caribs of whom
they were afraid.

The Caribs were darker in the skin, more warlike
and ruthless, a different Indian tribe, originating in
what is now Venezuela, which was gradually penetrat-
ing westwards along the curving sweep of the islands.
They were cannibals.

Columbus' friends belonged to a race in decline,
already condemned to death. In executing them the
Spaniards merely forestalled the Caribs. In fact they
killed them both. Those who came after Columbus
killed without stopping to investigate to which group
the Indians belonged. They killed with the sword,
cannon, whip, fire and specially trained bloodhounds.
They killed because the Indians proved unsuited to
hard work among the sugar-canes, which the Spaniards
introduced almost at once. By killing them off, the
Spaniards solved the problem of maintaining them, but,
having done that, where were they to get people to
work for them? There was only one answer.

Fifty years even before Columbus set sail from Palos,
the Portuguese had hit upon the idea of using African
negroes as slaves. In those days, the Portuguese were
far ahead of the rest of the world as explorers and
colonizers. They had established a number of fortified
trading stations along the lower west coast of Africa,
from which they made expeditions into the jungle to
capture black warriors who were of course well
accustomed to hard work in a tropical climate.

The first cargo of slaves reached Haiti in 1512, six
years after Columbus' death. This traffic grew at such
a pace that within a few decades it was reckoned that

about four thousand slaves were annually imported into the larger islands of the West Indies, among them Haiti. This traffic in " black ivory " acquired fantastic proportions in the 17th and 18th centuries, during which millions of blacks were bought and sold. By then, the slave traffic was no longer a Portuguese monopoly, in fact, it had mainly passed into other hands, those of the French, Dutch, English, Spaniards, even of the Danes. All seafaring nations had their share of it, and all shared in the responsibility for it— from the ordinary deckhand to the kings on their thrones. Every ship-owning country dabbled in the trade, but in the end it became predominantly English.

Then came the nineteenth century with its more humane ideas. In 1811 England took the lead and abolished slavery, and country after country followed her example. By that time, however, the West Indian market was saturated. In fact, the islands had become a black man's country ; so much so, that the abolition of slavery created a serious problem that led to bloodshed and revolt, mostly suppressed by the white colonists with a ruthless hand. But not on Haiti.

On Haiti the revolt was successful and that long before slavery was abolished. The Haitian revolt was caused by the French revolution, or rather was due to one idealistic negro having heard of the new conception of human rights, of liberty, equality and fraternity, and being sufficiently naive to imagine that that went for humans of all colours, and even for those outside the shadow of the guillotine. As a result, the negroes of Haiti threw off the yoke of the whites.

As far as the gold-thirsty Spaniards were concerned, the West Indian Islands had proved a great disappointment, and they were quick to abandon them when they found richer lands to plunder on the Central and South American mainland. As they moved out, other, less powerful nations moved in. To Haiti came the English and French, though the Spaniards still occupied the eastern part of the island which is to-day the republic of San Domingo, or Republica Dominicana, as it calls itself.

In 1629, the French threw the English out of their part of the island. By 1789, when the revolution broke out in Paris, Haiti was one of France's richest colonies. Its slaves were pronounced free, and one of them, Toussaint l'Ouverture, who was a highly gifted idealist, became so enthusiastic about the revolution that he proclaimed the whole island free and set up a republic on the French pattern. That was in 1801. By that time, however, the guillotine's appetite had been satiated and the trumpets of freedom had been muffled by a certain Napoleon Bonaparte. Napoleon had no wish to lose so profitable a source of income as was Haiti, and he pronounced Toussaint l'Ouverture a damned insurrectionary and despatched a force of 25,000 men under General Leclerc to the island.  Toussaint l'Ouverture was captured and sent to Paris where he died in prison. Leclerc reintroduced slavery, and Napoleon's brother-in-law was appointed governor. He had gone out there with the General, accompanied by his wife, Pauline.

The torch of freedom was now taken up by the negro general, Jean Jacques Dessalines, and the fight raged from one end of the island to the other across the savage mountains of Haiti. Then, Napoleon dismissed his brother-in-law and put General Richambeau in command, for the insurrection had to be put down whatever the cost. This was a time when kings and emperors quaked at the mere mention of Napoleon's name, and he was not going to allow some black slaves to defy him. So, reinforcements were sent to Haiti.

The war lasted a year, at the end of which the French army of 45,000 had been decimated partly by those blacks who neither gave nor asked for pardon, and by their powerful ally, yellow fever. Then, in 1804, Haiti was again, but this time properly, proclaimed an independent republic and Dessalines became its first president. He, however, could not be content with that title, and shortly afterwards he proclaimed himself emperor. Two years later he was killed by the mob for a tyranny worse than that to which any planter had ever subjected his slaves. He was succeeded by Henry Christophe, a former slave, a man who could neither read nor write, but all the same a natural genius.

Henry Christophe was a huge muscular man with a brutal face. Almost immediately strife broke out between him and his rival, Dessalines' former second-in-command during the war of liberation, the mulatto, Pétion. The conflict was resolved by their dividing up the island : Henry Christophe proclaimed himself king of the northern part which was then the more important, and Pétion became president of the southern half which was later to eclipse the northern completely, thanks to its possessing one of the best natural harbours in the West Indies, Port au Prince.

Henry Christophe was not the man to brook contradiction from any quarter, and he ruled as an absolute monarch, unrestrained dictator and despot. His people trembled before him, and deep within his own black heart he trembled before his people. In his morbid fear of them, that eventually turned into persecution mania, he built himself a gigantic fortress on top of one of the highest and most inaccessible mountains in the north of the island, dragging cannon all the way up to it, and there, to that eagle's nest, he retreated. To-day, it is counted among the wonders of the world, and by some held to surpass the pyramids of Egypt in majesty and in the labour it must have cost to build. There it was that he ended his days—by his own hand, with a bullet through his brain.

Is there not something familiar about that story : love of pomp, ruthless, merciless dictatorship, murder of political opponents, persecution mania, an eagle's nest as a refuge on an inaccessible mountain, and the final suicide when things collapsed ?

The development of this negro republic seems to have been unfortunate from the very start. Freed from the tyranny of the whites, the negroes passed under a yoke still more grievous that was set upon them by their fellows. The further history of Haiti in the nineteenth century is a continuing tale of bloodshed. The national debt grew enormously. Education ceased, individual greed appropriated whatever it could lay hands on, and corruption spread like wild-

fire. Banditry became commonplace, and none felt secure. So it continued right into our century, for in 1915 President Guillaume Sarn massacred his political opponents in prison, spiking them on the bayonets of his soldiers. He had to take refuge in the French Legation, but his subjects dragged him out and hacked him to pieces.

It seemed as though the black republic had not been able to catch the true rhythm of the melody of human rights and human ways. The millenium of which the poor negro slaves had dreamed when their chains dropped from them as a result of their own courageous fight, seemed as far off as ever. The end, however, was at hand, for Uncle Sam had watched and grown tired of the misdeeds of Haiti's rulers.

Two hours after the death of Guillaume Sarn, marines of the U.S.A. landed in every important bay, occupied all the strategic points and took over the government of the island for a period of twenty years. There remained a puppet government which said " Yes " to every order issued by the Americans. An attempted insurrection in 1918-20, led by a former bandit leader, was put down by the marines.

Meanwhile the American administrator set about putting the island and its accounts in order. During the twenty years of American rule the national debt was reduced from thirty-one to twenty million dollars ; roads, bridges, telephone and telegraph systems, irrigation and sanitary works were developed and improved ; agriculture was placed on a better footing, especially by the introduction of the sisal-agave as a crop.

In 1934 Uncle Sam handed over a greatly improved Haiti to a president who promised most earnestly to be very, very good in the future. Now, Haiti and its people are busy trying to be good, but nevertheless their age-old hatred of the white man for his superiority is still there just below the surface. It is perhaps, stronger than ever, for, as well as its positive results, the American occupation gave a tremendous stimulous to the Haitians' inferiority complex. You see, they had had more than a hundred years in which to prove to the white man that the blacks were his equal and themselves capable of building an ideal state that could serve as a model for the rest of the world, and they had not done it. All that had happened was that the white man had had to take over a bankrupt estate, bankrupt out of sheer neglect. They had done so, and, what was worse, they had put it on its feet again.

In 1945, the U.S.A. took 78.30% of Haiti's total exports and provided 83.77% of its imports. The figures will not have changed much since. Haiti knows that it cannot do without the U.S.A., and it hates the thought of being dependent more than any other part of the West Indies, just because it is the only country in which the inhabitants are all descended from slaves. Their forefathers staked their lives to fight for freedom and they won it; but then they and their children themselves turned it into a new and more grievous tyranny.

The majority of the population of Haiti are little better off than their ancestors were in 1804. The intelligent minority knows this and is ashamed of it, but it will not admit its shame to a white man. However, the best of them are working to change conditions and to raise the standard of living of the wretched majority. They have a long and arduous way to go.

CHAPTER XXIII

Past—Present—Future

The Foreign Minister received me in the palace on the Champs de Mars, a chalk-white building that gleams on dark evenings like some unreal fairy palace. It houses most of the government offices, and also the President who occupies the second storey.

Haiti's Foreign Minister is as black as ebony, a powerfully built, mild man with a soft voice that he never raises. He has the manners of a rural dean, is called Brutus, and is one of the best known Haitian poets. The poetry of Haiti can bear comparison with the best of French verse. There is an undertone of melancholy to it that on occasion can soar to fierce, savage heights. It is a refined version of the deeply serious, primitive song of the negroes of the Southern States.

The Foreign Minister was greatly interested in my plan to write about Haiti. He even put the matter before the President. It was, however, obvious that he was rather nervous lest I abuse his country's hospitality and write either condescendingly, or with actual malice, as had happened before when white journalists had come to describe this negro republic. The great man was apprehensive, but his position forbade him to show it. The real trouble was the number of books on Haiti which have taken the island's voodoo cult for their leit-motiv.

Altogether, this voodoo business is a difficult problem. Officially Haiti has to regard voodoo as something reprehensible, a relic of Congo paganism that has no place in a modern progressive republic; yet the idea of voodoo is very attractive to tourists and it is excellent propaganda which it would be irrational to drop. It is one of those attractions that give the American tourist that little shiver down the back that he or she loves to feel. In this respect, voodoo ranks along with the dried human heads of Panama and Ecuador. And then there is the fact that the monotonous rhythm of the voodoo drums is very close to the Haitians' conception of music, far closer than are the modern dances, foxtrot, rumba and tango, which, though they have absorbed part of the negroes' rhythm, can never be more than a very inferior substitute. Voodoo drums are Africa pure and unadulterated. They set every nerve vibrating in those whose great-grandfathers and grandfathers were brought from Africa as slaves some hundred years ago. They are, in fact, a ticklish problem.

I brought the subject up myself before the Minister had worked his way round to it. I promised him that though I would give some space to voodoo in what I would write, it would not be allowed to overshadow the modern side of progressive Haiti. Some space would *have* to be devoted to it, otherwise the picture would be false, for voodoo is Haiti's past, a thin red thread that runs on through the present into the nascent pattern of the future.

The modern progressive Haiti is best expressed in the central quarters of Port au Prince, where are the

President's palace and the other government buildings, luxurious offices, smart hotels, and modern cinemas, and in the airport with its busy traffic. There are the undeniably excellent technical and agricultural schools, where shiny black faces are bowed over tools and books ; there are the hospitals and petrol stations, such examples of modernity as the smart swimming pool at the Thorland Club, and Petionville's gay night-club. It rings the great cathedral with expensive shops and airy offices, and its highlight is, perhaps, the modern building of the tourist offices down by the port, where the tourist steamers tie up. There you will find Jean F. Brierre, Minister for Tourism, and his staff of smiling, cultured, helpful men and women.

That is one side of the picture. The other you can see if you go out on to the white road that leads in from the north. Down this comes an endless succession of picturesque women riding donkeys. They all have a red, green, or yellow kerchief tied round their heads, and the older ones chew away at the gnawed stem of a cutty-pipe. They are the Past coming into the market to do a deal with the Present. It is this mixture of past and present that makes Haiti the radiant, shocking experience that it is for tourists —and for journalists.

In Haiti's capital you will find modern houses cheek by jowl with rickety shacks built of packing cases and straw. There are smithies which are nothing more than a roof of palm leaves supported on four pillars under which sweating negroes, wearing nothing but a loin-cloth, swing their hammers in what is virtually the open air. Every other shack is a shop or business, but on a lilliputian scale. The record goes to a bar set up in an old packing case that had once brought a Buick from the U.S.A. One end of the packing case had been removed, a counter constructed at the other, and behind it a few shelves. That was all ; but it seemed to flourish.

Naked little boys play and do everything in the gutters. In scores of little workshops you can see busy tailors sitting at sewing machines so close together that their elbows touch. Light tropical suits and dresses hang from the roof above, like the flies in a theatre. Their blues and whites, browns and pinks, make a gay picture in the evening when the naked electric light bulbs are lit. In fact everything in Port au Prince makes you think of the theatre with its sharp contrasts and its light and shade.

There is no street lighting in Port au Prince. All the light comes from the bars and shops, and, once the shops in the main thoroughfares have closed, which they do early, darkness lies about the broad streets until daylight comes. A lighted shop window is quite unknown. In fact, as darkness falls, every door and window is closed with thick hurricane-shutters. It is only in the poor quarter of the town that the streets are thronged till late in the evening.

The women who come from the country sleep in the market-place, while their grey donkeys munch grass and straw. They sleep surrounded by their wares, head resting on a bundle of sugar-canes or a sack of sweet potatoes, ready for the morning when the housewives will come to do their shopping for another day. None thinks of going back to her home in the

In the country districts life is very primitive

La Citadelle : Henry Christophe's fortress

country until she has sold out. Some have come as many as fifty miles to the market Those who have more than a day's journey, spend the night in a sort of caravanserai under the open sky, or at the best with the thick crest of a mango or kapoc-tree to shelter them. Those who cannot afford to keep a donkey, walk striding along in bare feet with shoes perched on top of the basket containing the goods they are to sell. You see, in Port au Prince, no one is allowed to go barefoot. That would be undignified for a member of a civilized country, and any who do so are punished with imprisonment. When I learned that, I understood why the pilot and harbour police had looked so disapprovingly at us. Here was a luxury yacht, come all the way from Europe, and every man jack of the crew were wandering about the deck with bare toes bristling.

The Danish Consul told me that he once stopped his car away out in the country and offered to buy the heavy basket of oranges one of these market-women was balancing on her head. The woman had looked very thoughtful, then she had taken an extra deep pull at her pipe, and had said that she would sell the oranges for ten shillings. The Consul was most indignant and asked her whether she realized that he could buy the same number of oranges in the market itself for half that amount. The woman replied that she was quite aware of that and knew full well that, when she had walked the twenty-five miles or so that she still had to go, five shillings would be all she would get for her oranges. Her point was that, if she sold her oranges now, she would miss the pleasure of going to the town, and that she reckoned as being worth at least five shillings.

That these market women do enjoy their trips into town is only too obvious when you walk along the lines of them in the market-place. They squat there chattering away in their babbling lisping baby talk, that is called *patois* and officially held to be French. French! If you suddenly transplanted a Parisian to the market-place in Port au Prince, he would understand no more of what was being said than if he had been in the Calcutta bazaar.

The nearest description of their talk would be *spoken stenography*. The grammar is the simplest possible. The words are strung together and quite unrecognizable, for example *commeca*, which means "comment ça va." This tortured mutilated French is further adulterated by large admixtures of Spanish, African, and English words. That, plus the gutteral babbling intonation of the negro, so different from the clear French, means that there is very little of the original left to recognize or understand.

In the Haiti *patois* there are even rudiments of Swahili, which shows that some of the slaves had been taken the endless way across Africa, from the east of the continent to the "factories" on the west coast from which the slaves were shipped. Each Swahili word is a monument to inconceivable suffering endured long years ago.

Past and present meet in the hotels and restaurant of Haiti. A most lucrative encounter for the owners The prices charged in the hotels are those of the present, in particular, of New York: six to fifteen dollars a day with full board. The prices paid by the hotels and restaurants for meat, vegetables and labour, are those of the past. A woman kitchen-hand earns five dollars a month plus her food. A waiter gets two or three shillings a day and his food. It must be quite pleasant to own a tourist hotel in Port au Prince.

Past and present also meet in the realm of law and order. The police wear smart khaki uniforms of American cut and are armed with modern weapons; but the thief who breaks into your home does so stark naked, so that his black body is indistinguishable from the surrounding darkness, and he smears himself with grease to prevent you ever getting a grip of him. Night time in Port au Prince really deserves a chapter to itself.

In his *Journal* Columbus tells with amazement of the dumb dogs of Cuba and Haiti. I can assure him that that is all changed now. As soon as darkness falls the dogs lift up their voices. The air resounds with piercing and wailing howls. It is as though the darkness were swarming with ghosts unable to find peace or rest. If the howling of the dogs ever ceases, it is immediately replaced by the screeching and moaning of cats that seem to be perched on every roof and every fence. Sometimes the two concert, and then it is like thousands of evil spirits howling and moaning in the moonlight.

It is only when the chorus of piercing cock-crows begins with the dawn that the dogs and cats fall silent, but then the women-hawkers strike up their monotonous long drawn out howls. That is the signal for the general hubbub of motor-car horns, bells and braying to begin—and so another day starts, and you rise sleepily from your bed and go to try the shower-bath which won't work till you have cleaned its holes with a darning needle.

The Foreign Minister put a car at my disposal. With me came a representative of the tourist ministry, a young poet, and an American negro sculptor Richmond Barthé, and *his* adjutant, the poet Casseus. Barthé had been brought over to make two statues of Haiti's national hero, Toussaint l'Ouverture, and, Heaven knows they are wanted, for the local talent has not yet got beyond tame imitations of the most appalling *plat-de-menage* style. Barthé was also to model a relief of the President for a new series of small coins, the first Haiti will have had since 1907. His adjutant, Casseus, was there to inspire him.

Casseus' normal occupation was writing poems and fairy-tales. However, the President had dismissed his Foreign Minister four days previously and replaced him with the poet Brutus, who had in his turn changed the Tourist Minister and given that portfolio to the poet, Brierre, who had planted several other poets in his ministry.

My guide was delighted with our tour. He had never been in those parts of the country before, and plied the others with questions about what we were seeing. Thanks to my having read up the history, geography, and studied the map of Haiti, I was usually able to tell him.

The first stretch of the road was a really superb highway, but a mile or two out from the capital it suddenly turned into an unmetalled country road full of holes and littered with loose stones.

Behind Port au Prince lies a huge plain. Flat as a pancake it extends far inland until two chains of mountains squeeze it into a point, giving it the shape of a triangle. The plain is planted with sugar-cane, sisal-agave, and maize. People were busy in the sisal plantations as we passed. Moving up and down along those long rows of bristly plants, they were tying the leaves into bundles and carrying them off on donkeys' backs, in lorries, or trucks running on narrow-gauge railways, to the factories where hundreds of smiling women pound and wash and dry the long tough fibres that are hidden in the thick leaves, fibres of which one day ropes and sandals, sun-hats and handbags, will be made.

Ahead were the mountains. Seen from this side they are naked and brown. On the north side more rain falls, and also Port au Prince has not yet stretched its tentacles so far. There used to be thick forests here, so lovely that it made Columbus fill his *Journal* with more poetry than facts. But that has all been ruthlessly cut down, giving the rains free play. The thin layer of fertile top-soil has been washed off the mountain sides and swept away down the streams and rivers out into the sea, leaving naked rock protruding everywhere. The old, old, story of waste.

Who here thinks of manuring? As far as I could see, none. The wind was sending a golden-brown dust, as fine as flour, swirling round the car. It penetrated everywhere, into our noses, eyes, ears, mouths, and cameras. We tied our handkerchiefs over the lower

half of our faces, as though we were boys playing at being Tuaregs. Our hair was powdered a greyish-brown. Those we overtook or met on the road, hastened to turn their own and their donkey's head away from us, and held their noses as we dashed past. The dust was so fine that it remained hanging like mist in the air, and from up on the mountainside we could trace our passage across the plain by the dust-cloud along the road.

Every now and again we would drive through a village : pure Africa. Just a collection of straw huts lying in the sunshine, each with a hole in the side for a door, a hard earthen floor on which were one or two wretched beds made of banana leaves laid over a frame of sticks, but no other furniture. Mangy dogs, scraggy hens, and small black pigs were running in and out of the doorways.

Everything is on a small scale out here in the country. The people themselves are small or short-legged ; the goats, pigs, donkeys, bananas, oranges, everything is smaller than normal, a sure sign of inbreeding, degeneration, and inappropriate diet. Out here, the elegant white government palace seemed a very long way away.

Occasionally we would pass a cabin with five or six coffee bushes round it. It was the coffee season and there was a festive air about the brilliant red of the berries, only the berries were horribly sparse.

Haiti comes high up the list of the large coffee exporters, yet there are no coffee-plantations on the island. On the other hand, there are perhaps a hundred thousand little gardens in which coffee bushes blossom and produce berries, and round about in the woods are wild bushes whose berries are also gathered and laid out to dry on small cement floors in front of the straw huts along the roadside and far up the valleys.

Not till the coffee is dry, is it taken down to the buyers, who dry it again on huge expanses of cement, and there all impurities and dust are picked out by women and girls who squat round it, each with a little heap of coffee in front of her. After that, the beans are picked and sorted according to size and colour. That is how Haiti's exports of coffee are gathered together : a sort of mosaic of countless tiny stones.

The best beans are the large ones of yellowish-green colour. The small deformed ones fetch the least, and these are mostly exported to Amsterdam, from where, I suspect, quite a number find their way farther north to certain restaurants that I know. That, however, is perhaps not so important, for the experts maintain that what makes good coffee is rather the method of preparing it, than the quality of the beans.

One of these experts once entertained two Scandinavian importers in his home. He gave them coffee and asked them for their opinion of its quality. They let the brown fluid slide over their tongues, rolled their eyes appreciatively, and pronounced it the best grade of the best crop, etc., etc. The expert then, somewhat tactlessly, told them that it was made from sweepings from the cement floors of his warehouse, but *well* made.

Coffee beans are at their best when they have been in store for two or three years. After that, they begin to lose their taste, and after fifteen to twenty years they are dry and worthless. New coffee is too damp and has a tendency to get mouldy. What coffee needs between the time it is harvested till it is sold, is sunshine and still more sunshine. All over Haiti there are great cement yards on which beans are spread to absorb the sunlight and warmth.

The U.S.A. and Holland are Haiti's two best customers for its coffee.

The banana plantations alongside the road were a great temptation with the enticing green of their leaves. If only it had been possible to stretch out in their cool shade for a while, for the sun was blazing down upon the road without mercy. The car, however, went on and on, dragging its great train of dust through the countryside.

The whole population of Haiti seemed to be on the move. The roads and paths were all lined with women, women on foot, women on donkeys, women with bundles on their heads, and women who had halted for a moment to drink and bathe their feet in the cold water of some mountain torrent. When occasionally we rattled across the loose planks of a bridge, down below we would see women squatting by the river washing clothes, while naked children splashed in the swift eddies. Some of the women had modestly kept their clothes on, others were bare to the waist, and they all chattered away and laughed out loud at the least little thing.

So, too, do the women who sit at regular intervals along the streets of the villages and beside the main roads. They sit there behind a soap box or a straw tray, on which they have arranged some oranges, bananas, sugar-canes, sickly sweet home-made confectionery, bread, or almost boiling Coca-Cola and " seven up." I never saw any of them sell anything. But, perhaps, those little stalls were merely pretexts to enable them to sit quietly there and see life pulsing past, and to have a comfy chat with their fellows as they came and went.

Our dust settled thick on their bread and cakes.

When evening falls, these women light flickering little torches on their stalls. To drive past in a car, is like driving down a road lined on either side with will-o'-the-wisps, each of which for a fleeting instant lights up a white smile, a pair of rolling eyes, and a glaring yellow head-cloth. Strange flowers to find growing along the edge of a ditch.

The Haiti of the past is, as I have said, just Africa ; but we were heading for the Haiti of the future. Two and a half miles from the frontier with the neighbouring state of San Domingo, is a village built by Haiti's President, Dumarsais Estimé. He built it because Señor Trujillo, the dictator of San Domingo, had built one on the other side of the frontier. Señor Trujillo has built several villages up and down the country, but that on the frontier was a show place. And that, of course, called for an answer.

There is something unhealthy about this rivalry. These new villages are fairy-tale affairs : they have first-rate sanitation, magnificent bungalows of which most Europeans would be justifiably proud, excellent hospitals and shops, etc., etc. But—the gulf between them and the normal Haitian villages is too enormous to be crossed in one jump. You cannot make people

go from the Middle Ages straight into the twentieth century, from the jungle of the Congo to suburban Europe in one bound. Mankind is not sufficiently elastic to traverse the centuries at that speed without losing its breath and balance. You would have thought that it must have been obvious that any such experiment was doomed to failure that sought to take the bare-footed inhabitants of straw huts and put them along with their faithful train of geese, pigs, dogs and hens, into modern bungalows with bathroom and w.c., where they would have an electric cooker instead of an open fire on the ground.

It cost roughly £150,000 to build Belladére, which the government responsible hailed with a flood of speeches and panegyric brochures. It was created by a stroke of the pen of a newly-elected President who also decided to spend £1,000,000 on a great exhibition at Port au Prince. That is the sort of man the President is. Within a short time of his election, badly printed pictures of him in tail coat and white tie were distributed all over the country to be hung up in every public meeting place, every home and every shop.

New notes are being sounded in Haiti; but to the ear of a European they have a familiar, unpleasant ring.

Would it not have been better to have spent that £150,000 on expanding the schools, on educating the poor people so as to make them able to accept and appreciate better conditions some time in the future? Would not the million pounds that are to be devoted to the exhibition be better spent cleaning up some of Haiti's appalling slums? The contrast between the magnificent palaces of the exhibition and the dark wretched negro huts that will stand in their shade, will be crass indeed.

When the journalists go to Haiti for the exhibition, more than one, I am sure, will notice these lights and shades and be more interested in them than in the gay posters illustrating progress under the present President. Some may even notice that the President's white-clad ministers receive £5 a day, while the man who sweeps the marble steps down which they walk, and the women who grade the coffee Haiti exports, must content themselves with two or three shillings a day.

Nobody yet seems to be quite clear who is to live in Belladére, or on what those who do are to live. For the time being, the village stands empty. On its outskirts, people have made themselves very much at home, in straw huts with earthen floors. All the same, we drank to the village's future in champagne in the elegant offices of the local administration, standing beneath a large coloured photograph of the President arrayed in all his glittering orders and blue riband across his chest.

" Haiti needs a *strong* man," said Casseus, looking up at the photograph.

All right ! It has got one.

I went outside to take photographs. On the fringe of the village I came across a team of navvies levelling the ground for yet another ' ideal " building. Black as ebony, or coffee brown, their muscular arms and shoulders rose and fell rhythmically as they swung their picks and shovels. Up-to-date lorries loaded the earth and rubble and drove away full. A tractor was chugging away in the distance. Nearby was a flaming camp fire over which a woman was cooking food for the men, a little open fire built on the ground in front of a straw hut. The men were singing. It was a mono-tonous, guttural tune that continually repeated the same excitant motive, a song straight from the African jungle, a song to be sung to the accompaniment of drums, such as you can hear when naked negroes are loading a big steamer on the Liberian coast, or when paddlers are driving a canoe through the brown eddies of the Congo, or when men dance by the light of a full moon deep within the heart of Africa. That song the slaves had brought with them. Unchanged, Africa is to-day singing the same old song as it helps to build the new Haiti, or at any rate, its President's dream for the future, a dream of cement, mirror-glass and shiny tiles.

That picture gripped and moved me more than anything else on the whole journey; for, there, within the one frame, was grouped Haiti's past, present, and future.

CHAPTER XXIV

The Reverse of the Medal

THE white man on a visit to Haiti encounters one
great difficulty : the ordinary Haitian in the street or
on the country roads regards all whites as Americans.
He knows, too, that in America there are some whites
who do not treat the negroes decently. However
closely the country may officially be linked to the
U.S.A., however friendly and polite the official utter-
ances, deep below the surface there seethes and bubbles
a real hatred of the whole race that has produced the
Ku-Klux-Klan. It is the burning, suppressed hatred
of the underdog, of the subdued and subjected. On
Haiti, the people's hatred of the whites goes so far as
to include, or at any rate to raise an invisible barrier
against, all who are of mixed blood. Officially, of
course, there is no such barrier, but every day hundreds
of little episodes, remarks and actions, bear witness
to its existence. Let me tell you about one.

I had expressed a desire to see a dance while I was
in the island. I had meant, of course, a folk dance, a
real native affair with drums and bamboo instruments.
Whether it was a delicate snub on the part of the tourist
department, I don't know. It may merely have been
that they wanted to show me that there was *civilized*
dancing on an island inhabited by people darker in the
skin than I was ; I don't know. Whichever it was,
they drove me out to a little village in the country

where some festivity was to take place. The Mayor of the village invited me to his home, where all the other village dignitaries had assembled for cocktails and afternoon dancing to a military band in spotless uniforms.

If the intention had been to give me a gentle reprimand, they were unfortunate to have chosen this village. At least, I can't believe that they had been *so* deep that they had thought they would confront me with a caricature of my own race.

The mayor was a political upstart, young, slim, with shifty restless eyes. He first introduced me to his wife. She was a lovely creature, an entrancing little doll dressed in a picturesque and smart adaptation of folk-costume to modern dress. That done he told her to fetch two glasses of beer. It was just as though he had spoken to his dog. Then he took her by the shoulder and gave her a sharp push, to indicate that he wanted the beer brought quickly. When she had returned with two silver goblets brimming with ice-cold " schlitzbeer," she went and sat down in a corner of the room, where she stayed gazing, like one fascinated, at her husband.

I was speaking French, but the mayor intended by hook or by crook to talk English, a language he only too obviously did not know. Haltingly he told me how he had become mayor, how he had purposely worked to make himself popular among the labourers and agricultural workers. He gave me a cynical, brutal lesson on how to do it, and ended by saying : " And now I am the most respected man in the whole commune."

246

At one point, his guests stopped, seemingly un-
certain what it was I really wanted. "Dance!" he
shouted at them. And they danced.

Then he turned to me and said, "Dance with my
wife!", at the same time summoning her with a nod.
We danced, while his shifty eyes followed us. A
moment later he interrupted the proceedings and told
me to take some photographs of his guests dancing.
I got my Leica and pretended to be taking photograph after photograph, but did not take a single one.
It would not have been fair. Here were men and
women, members of a race which has one of the best
senses of rhythm and music in the world, and yet they
were dancing stiffly round the room, trailing their
feet like unwilling pupils at a dancing class. Not only
that, but the women were dressed in the latest patterns
from *Harpers Bazaar* and *Vogue*, magnificent lithe
negresses dolled up in the latest tomfoolery from
Paris, designed for those women who must make a
sensation at whatever cost. The men, muscular and
narrow-hipped, were masquerading in white and blue
tropical suits and bow ties. They danced with stiff
left arms, holding their partner at the regulation
distance, and trying to engage her in light conversation, while they themselves were grimly serious.

It was like a reception in a legation. Or, almost.
Little fingers jutted out stiffly at right angles to cups,
some of them with green nails. All the women were
wearing hats. Foxtrot: one-two-three and four-five.
You would have been doubled up with laughter, if
the whole scene had not been so hopelessly sad and
dismal.

Here was an entire negro people that had had the the chance to fashion its own country, its own traditions and its own justification. They had fought for that chance, shed their blood to get it, a century and a half ago. And what has been the result? A little of it was to be seen there in the mayor's home, where the what-not with its knick-knacks and the red plush chairs had been pushed back against the walls, so that the village dignitaries could tread their dreary measures under the shifty eyes of the mayor, who was wearing a light blue silk scarf draped diagonally across his white shirt. Its gold fringe hung down below his jacket at the back.

Having won their freedom, these people have now voluntarily bowed their shoulders under the yoke of convention, in the naive belief that the white man is in all respects the most favoured being in the world. Unable to discriminate, without even stopping to think, they are slavishly copying everything from their hated former masters. The result, or one of them, was that dance at the house of the mayor of that little village. There are plenty of others, things which make the white tourist smile contemptuously—and that it is so, is a thousand pities, for with that excellent human material something quite new could have been made, a happy country which would have cared nothing for the mistakes or the ridiculous side of the white races.

What wonderful material they would have been for the true statesman and idealist to fashion ! A people with none of the shortcomings and poses of the white man; men and women as credulous and as prone to laughter as children, who were enchanted

The coffee beans are dried in the sun on huge cement floors,

and then they are carefully sorted and graded

at their escape from the bonds of slavery. With such people, surely one could have built the millennium.

But, instead of idealists, they were given imitators to govern them: generals with patent-leather boots and trailing swords, egoists and people crazy for power, and their country was built up on the principle *" so ein Ding muss Ich auch haben! "* That maleable material was at once poured into the rigid moulds of the white man's civilization and hastily set up for view, without anyone taking the time even to remove impurities or smooth the surface.

Now, those who set the tone dance with stiff faces, afraid to give way to the desire that *must* be within them, the desire to throw aside those cramping Paris dresses and to hurl themselves into a whirling spell-binding dance to the accompaniment of drums and bamboo flutes.

" Every child in the commune knows me," said the mayor, righting his tie. " Every citizen knows and loves me."

At that moment a lad in rags was thrown down the steps. The music had attracted him, like light a moth. I had seen him standing there outside with his arms in the air, his hips swaying, his eyes closed, while his bare feet stamped out the rhythm on the cool marble floor of the porch. Then he was thrown out.

"Take a photo of us. A group. And then one of the new cars over there," ordered the mayor, and I obediently walked down the steps and got my camera ready.

" Come over here, you! " called the mayor to five well-dressed, but very light-coloured mulattoes who were just on the point of leaving.

"No!" said the mulattoes, turning their backs on us. "Yesterday you refused our company, so, to-day, we won't be photographed with you." And they walked away.

A drunk man from the village came and wanted to join us. He thought he would like to be in the group. The mayor turned on him fiercely, and his falsetto voice screeched as he poured out an angry flood of patois. The drunk insisted. He was removed by two policemen.

"Now take your picture!" said the mayor. He never spoke a sentence that hadn't an exclamation mark at the end.

I took the photograph and left.

Ahead of me walked the little group of mulattoes. They were squabbling. I was too far away to catch every word they said, but what they were talking was pure, resonant French. I could not help feeling tremendous sympathy for the light-coloured in this country, for one day they may well come to hate their fathers and to despise their mothers who brought them into the world without a home, a world where they are looked down upon by the whites and ostracized by the blacks. Yes, even in the free negro republic of Haiti, for there they have faithfully copied each one of the thousands of shortcomings of the white man, including his racial hatreds.

If you drive through the woods of Haiti on a Saturday evening after the sun has set, you will probably hear above the hum of the engine the occasional sound of distant drums. If you drive by day along the dusty roads far from the capital you may be lucky enough to see a tree—it will be one of the largest round about—from whose thick branches dead hens, clothes and fruit dangle on strings. *Voodoo*.

People have written thrillers about Haiti's voodoo. You may have read one or two with their tales of human sacrifice and the murder of inquisitive whites who have sneaked up too near. There was once an American writer who spent a few weeks in an island off Haiti. There he came across an old crone whose appearance was most dramatic. He bought an expensive and magnificent gown in Port au Prince, dressed her up in it, and put a cheap tin crown on her head, and so photographed her from every angle, and wrote the most murderous exciting tales about her. The old crone, of course, was highly delighted with the gown and crown, but she hadn't the least idea why they had been given to her. Her picture appeared in the American press with the underline: " The Voodoo Queen."

That is not just the malicious invention of a jealous journalist. It was told to me by the island's greatest expert on voodoo history, ceremonial and music, Dr. Louis Maximilien, when I visited him at Cape Haiti. He told me the story with a wry smile and dismissed it with a shrug. Dr. Maximilien has one of the finest collection of pre-Columbian ceramics in private ownership, and also a thing that is quite unique, one of the " pipes " the Indians used for smoking tobacco at the time when Columbus first discovered the plant. It is hollow and shaped like the fork of a branch. In those days, the Indians method of smoking was to stick the two short ends up their nostrils, and so inhale the smoke from tobacco leaves burning on a fire.

Dr. Maximilien has written a book about voodoo, a scientific work. According to him, the talk about human sacrifice is all nonsense. As a rule, it is either a black or a white hen that is killed. And, if an inquisitive stranger should appear on the scene, he is thrown out and conducted a short distance on his way back to whence he came, in exactly the same way as happens when an outsider forces his way into a private dance in the village hall. That is all there is to it.

However, the voodoo cult is in itself of enormous interest, because it is the old pagan superstition of Africa which was brought to the islands by the first of the negro slaves, and there it took root and there it still flourishes. In the course of years, it has borrowed from Christianity so much, that to-day it is the strangest mixture of paganism and Catholicism, just as are *macumba* in Brazil and *obi* in Jamaica. All three cults have gone through the same process independently of each other, and the same is true of all places where large numbers of negro slaves have been gathered. Whether in Brazil or on Haiti, it is the same primitive jungle instruments that are used : the drum and the bamboo flute.

The negroes needed something round which they could group themselves ; they needed recourse to powers who could stand over them and help them in their sufferings. This they had in their old pagan religion, and as the years passed it became adulterated with little bits of Christianity, until in the end, the old gods were inextricably mixed up with the new saints against a background of jungle magic and exorcism in which the names of Jesus and Mary crop up every now and then. This they had and have, and also their dances. They dance themselves into religious ecstasy to the monotonous rhythm of drums.

The dance is the negro's natural means of expression ; rhythm a component of his soul. But both his dance and his music are as far removed from the European conception of those two things as black is from white.

The adherents of the voodoo cult go to Mass as regularly as any of the faithful. In fact, theirs is a burning faith, greater than that of most ; yet, for them, it is still too little. Their voodoo ceremonies they regard as coming under the church, as a sort of secret lodge for more intensive cultivation of the heavenly powers, a freemasonry whose initiation and other ceremonies are secret and complicated.

The signs with which voodoo altars and meeting places are decorated are an amazing mixture of pagan symbols and motives borrowed from contemporary Christianity. Before a ceremony begins, an artist traces an intricate pattern on the cement floor of the lodge, using white flour. It includes snakes, a cross, sailing boats and stars, cabalistic signs, hearts, crowns of thorns, and cows. Backwards and forwards across it all goes the dance, growing wilder and wilder as the drums beat on. Down on to it drips blood from the sacrificial hens and goats, and in the end it is all rubbed out by women in hysterical ecstasy reaching down as they dance in ever wilder swirls.

This extraordinary mixture of paganism and christianity gives the imaginative negro a religious sexual satisfaction which the Christian Church, whose ceremonial is constructed for the mentality of the white races, is not able to offer. Voodoo, in fact, is an outlet, a safety-valve that normally is of the greatest importance.

The adherents of voodoo are to be found all over Haiti, from the deep valleys of the interior to the main streets of Port au Prince, and among people of all classes. The ordinary person makes no bones about it; the more intellectual conceal the fact out of a false sense of shame. When I used to lie awake in my bunk in the *Santa Maria*, as we lay off the coast of Haiti, I would often hear the dull beat of drums coming from off the shore through the depths of the night, and then I would go up on deck and see distant fires glowing on the mountainsides. Sometimes, the thump, thump of the drums would grow so strong and loud that it drowned the noise of motor-car horns and barking dogs from the nearby town by the shore, and those drums would make the blood course more quickly in my veins.

ogoun feraille

Gradually, the lights in the town would be extinguished. The full moon would rise blood-red above blue mountains and make the lagoons glitter where the water lapped the shore. The thump thump of the drums would rise and fall like the swell running gently under *Santa Maria*, and the water along her sides would be sparkling and phosphorescent, as though voodoo fires had also been lit deep down below among the dusky coral. At such times, I would think of that reception in the house of the village mayor; and the more I thought of it, the less inclined I felt to smile or laugh at him or it. For me, the white-uniformed brass band, and those foxtrots and solemn faces, were but a façade hiding the profound tragedy that is the inner division of Haiti.

CHAPTER XXV

A Mad Emperor's Eyrie

THE north coast of Haiti is quite different from its south coast. You notice that as soon as you cross the watershed up in the thin cool air of the mountains. Rain falls on the northern slopes of those mountains and so they are covered with thick luxuriant jungle forest, while the southern slopes are bare and burned up by the sun. Even the houses in the villages are different. Those on the southern slopes are rickety affairs of straw laid over a crude framework of wood, and roofed with palm leaves. Those in the north are built of mud and clay, and are properly thatched. Their walls are painted, the usual colour scheme being a golden ochre with an edging of white round the doors and windows. Not only that, but they *have* doors that can be opened and shut, and neat curtains at the window openings. These signs of greater prosperity, and the more solid construction of the houses themselves, are certain indications of a different climate. Here, within the one country, is confirmation of the theory that a colder climate makes people more active and enterprising.

In this part of the island there still remain patches of the jungle that so entranced Columbus. What you see is a thick tangle of tree-tops of every size and shade of green; broad lobed leaves of banana plants

The old-fashioned sugar-mills have their own beauty

Cape Haiti, near where Columbus lost *Santa Maria*

and yams, the fine leaves of mahogany and kapoc trees, whose mighty trunks glisten silvery-gray amongst the others; and here and there a tree entirely covered by creepers of various kinds. The creepers weave themselves through its crown and droop down over the side. Some have lilac flowers, others white, and when the tree itself puts out red blossom, you understand how Columbus, who was more sailor than botanist, wrote of trees that bore different kinds of leaves and flowers on the one stem.

Above the jungle tower the mountains that rise up steeply from the flat sugar fields of the coastal plain. Among the highest peaks drift blue-grey clouds, that now settle and obliterate them, then slowly move on, leaving here and there a little swab of cloud sticking to a cleft or jutting rock. Out over the sea, white cumulus clouds are lazily sailing before the gentle Trades. Behind them, the sky is clear and resplendently blue. The mountains are so grim and grave, that they barely seem to belong to the same landscape.

The natural line of the highest mountain of them all is broken by the defiant profile of a building on its slope. Here it was, at a height of over 3,000 feet, where the air is chill and birds of prey seldom go, that mad Henry Christophe built his castle, La Citadelle. It is like a clenched fist that menaces both heaven and earth, a monument to the lengths to which persecution mania will drive a man. Beside it Hitler's " eagle's nest " in the Bavarian Alps is a plaything.

Henry Christophe's castle has been compared to the pyramids of Egypt, but to build the pyramids on the flat desert must have been child's play compared

I

with the herculean effort it must have cost to drag
dressed stones, mortar and heavy bronze cannon, up
three thousand feet of almost inaccessible mountain
to build a fortress for a mad negro monarch. With
the range of cannon in the days when it was built, that
gigantic fortress must have been well-nigh impreg-
nable, especially as its storerooms could hold enough
to last its garrison for years, while an ingenious
system for catching and storing rainwater was able
to supply all their needs.

The situation of La Citadelle is so remote that but
few ever visit it. All the roads stop at the foot of the
mountain. After that, if you wish to reach it, you must
laboriously make your way on foot for seven miles
along a steeply rising path that is just round stones
or slippery mud, while the sun bakes down and the
air hangs still, with seldom a tree to provide any shade.
If you want to drink, you must carry water with you ;
and you will need a lot, for the sweat pours off you
as though you were standing under a shower bath,
making your clothes cling to your body.

It is possible to hire a small skinny horse to carry
you up. It will set its feet as securely as a mountain
goat ; but even if you can overcome your scruples
and decide to burden the poor beast, you will discover
on your return that you are just as sore as if you had
walked, only in another place. Those who ride up
in the morning, are usually found taking their evening
meal standing at the bar. Also, those who walk reach
the top first, and they too, are the first down. I know
that, for I started out from the valley level with an
American and his wife who had hired horses. I had

been at the top half an hour before I saw them come limping up to the gateway, their legs curved outwards as though they were still astride the saddle.

The starting-point for La Citadelle is the little village of Millot at the foot of the mountains. You cannot see the fortress from the village, but you do get a wonderful view of the smaller pleasure abode Christophe had built here in the valley. *Sans Souci* he called it, and what a tragic misnomer that was, for if ever a man was tormented by care and worries, it was this negro king in his latter years. Here the black " roi soleil " held revels of barbarian magnificence for his officers. A bare twenty years after the French Revolution had guillotined the splendour-loving courtiers of Versailles—as well as giving the impetus that set Haiti's slaves free—here they were aping the luxury of the French court in its every aspect, while thousands of slaves worked themselves to death dragging stones up the mountainside. Less than ten years after they had cast off the yoke of their white masters, a small minority of negro slaves was already using their freedom to oppress their less gifted and less enterprising fellows. And Haiti witnessed orgies of cruelty.

Every now and again you come across a stretch of the path that has been paved. It has not been done with any intention of easing the climb. Not at all, the stones are triangular or hexagonal and set in the most uncomfortable manner ; their purpose was to let those in the listening posts in the fortress hear the sound of horse's hooves in plenty of time to man the defences.

Wild orange trees lean out over the path. If you reach up and pluck one of their golden fruits, bite a hole in the skin and suck, you will find it sour and bitter, but marvellously refreshing. At long intervals the path flattens out into a little plateau, where there will be a little house with the inevitable stretch of cement for drying coffee in front. Otherwise, everything is virgin and uncultivated. Here and there a mountain stream chuckles among the thick bushes. Lizards scuttle across the path. Parrots screech. A humming-bird hovers for two or three seconds in front of a flame-coloured flower, while it sucks out the honey with its thin long beak. A snake makes its leisurely way across the slabs of rock, but it is not poisonous. There are no poisonous snakes in Haiti. The only venomous creatures in the island are centipedes, scorpions, and bird spiders.

In places the clay between the slabs of rock is as slippery as soap, bringing it home to you that the path was made for mountain goats and not for men. The sweat pours down your back, and you curse and swear that it cannot possibly be worth the effort; but then suddenly your foot strikes something hard, and, bending down, you discover an old bronze cannon covered with moss and jungle plants. It is French, a good hundred and fifty years old, and ornamented with twirls and squiggles, a piece that any museum would be proud to own. A little farther on you come across a score of rusty cannon-balls lying half-buried in the mud. Perhaps, some sweating slaves dropped them there when they heard that Henry Christophe had taken his own life out of fear of the ring of enemies with which he felt himself surrounded day and night, fear of the whispering voices he heard everywhere, of the hoarse voices that reached him out of the night calling for vengeance, the voice of conscience that finally drove him mad.

Work stopped on the fortress the day Christophe died. They buried him in the middle of the great courtyard, covered the grave over with a great slab of cement, and left the fortress to be overgrown and for time to crumble. It was, in fact, never properly finished.

On and on you climb, but still you can see no sign of the fortress. You can only picture it, as you saw it from near the coast, twelve miles away. Then, as you round a shoulder, there it suddenly is five hundred yards from where you stand. The sight of it takes your breath away.

It is overwhelmingly majestic and blunt. Menacing and severe, it is like something out of the sinister history of the Middle Ages. The north tower of the bastion rises up like the sheer stern of a ship, piercing the clouds that drive round it on either side to unite again at its foot. The grey-brown walls are of tremendous thickness. Its proportions are gigantic, but nevertheless in perfect harmony. Architecturally it is a fine and virile piece of work. The man who built it may have been mad, but he was also a genius. You admit now that it was well worth the arduous climb, and you forget your aching muscles and wet clothes— and set off to explore the inside.

You can wander for hours in the long, dark corridors and galleries, into which but a meagre light comes through the embrasures in the massive walls. The trees outside give a greenish tint to the sunlight, creating an illusion of unreality and making you feel as though you were in some fairy realm beneath the sea. Small bushes now grow out of the loopholes, grass grows in every cranny, and damp and moss have covered the stone walls with a layer of green slime. Behind those great walls the cannons stand one beside the other, like grey elephants in their stalls, tethered to the stone floor by an iron rail on which they once were able to swing so that they commanded most of the valleys deep down below.

And what valleys those are! If you climb up to the top of the tower and stand there bowed against the icy wind that comes howling out of the dark clouds, you can see for miles out across the mountains of Haiti and the low land along the coast, and from within the gloom among the clouds see how the cloud's shadows race on across the countryside only in the end to give up their struggle with the fresh Trades and brilliant sunshine, and disappear above the white edging of the coral reef. The whole north coast of Haiti is spread out below like a map. There, deep beneath me was *Santa Maria*, a mere speck of white, a gull that had settled on the blue water of the bay out by Cape Haiti.

As well as the great fortress itself, Henry Christophe had built a number of small forts on some of the lower mountain tops round about, at such points where they could cover other valleys and the dead ground which the cannon in La Citadelle could not command.

The whole roofing of the citadel was designed as a catchment area for rain-water which was led along pipes down into huge cisterns in the lower storeys. The living quarters were shot-proof, and in one of the corner towers there was even a billiard room, a round room with a vaulted domed ceiling, which is now the duty room of the caretakers. Every tourist must go there and write his name in a book before making the tour of the citadel.

Everywhere there are piles of cannon-balls of all sizes, thousands and hundreds of thousands of them piled up in great pyramids and oval heaps. There are enough for several years of siege and warring, yet none of the cannon were ever fired. No enemy ever came, and the only shot to ring out there was the one that shattered Henry Christophe's skull and so drew a gory line under that chapter of Haiti's bloody history.  Out in the great yard is the cement block, shaped like a house and painted white, that marks the modest grave of a mad negro king whom they buried right in the centre of the marvel his genius had created. Tourists always go and stand in front of it to be photographed ; then they scrawl their names and addresses on its white surface. That done, they pinch a cannonball and send it rolling down the mountain side, or else play skittles with it in the long galleries, scaring the lizards.

It is at night, when all the tourists have long since returned safely to the valley and the citadel lies bathed in the light of the moon that gleams palely through the gaps in the storming clouds, that the citadel should be seen. As the moonbeams play on the yard-thick walls in endless variety of light and shade, the innate cruelty of the place comes to life in squeaking bats, and the evil thoughts that dwell there flit noiselessly on owls' wings out of peepholes and embrasures that are black like the empty eye-sockets in a whitened skull. Then, the restless giant form of mad Henry Christophe paces the dark galleries, stopping to look out over the valley, only to resume his pacing up and down, up and down ; and an icy breath of fear swirls down over the valley and the jungle, and the air is filled with the sighs and groans of tormented black slaves labouring up the mountain with stones to build La Citadelle for a mad negro king.

CHAPTER XXVI

Journey's End

WHILE I was forced to take to motor cars, Shank's
pony, and other earth-bound means of transport in
order to get from place to place and see what I
wanted to see in Haiti, *Santa Maria* was most of the time
weather-bound in a cosy little creek near Port de Paix,
where Columbus had also lain waiting for the weather
to clear and let him slip through the capricious seas
of the strait between Haiti and Tortuga. In the end,
she was able to move on and we sailed her along to
Cape Haiti, where she was riding uneasily at anchor
behind the coral reef on which the first *Santa Maria*
came to grief on Christmas Eve, 1492.

The waves were breaking white over the reef in the
north east. We got past that all right, and so could
have Columbus, only by that time his officers and crew
had grown a little slack ; they thought that they knew
conditions better than they did, that there was nothing
to it in putting in and out of small bays, avoiding coral
reefs and slipping into the safety of river mouths.
But there is, even though there is nothing specially
complicated about putting in to this particular bay.
Anyone accustomed to sailing among reefs and rocks
would find it just a routine job.

Round about midnight on 24th December, 1492,
everyone on Columbus' *Santa Maria* had turned in.
The breeze had died away momentarily, and there

was only a gentle swell that was scarcely able to lift the heavy caravels. They were steering for a promontory which they called *Punta Santa*, the sacred point, and as the sea was calm the helmsman had handed over to one of the ship's boys and lain down for a snooze himself. There was a westerly current. The course was set out exactly. The moon was new. *Niña* was in the lead with *Santa Maria* a short way astern. The waves were just lazily breaking on the coral reef to starboard of her.

It was a proper night in which to rest after the last few days which had been hard and stirring. After standing a while at the rail chatting with the mate, Juan la Cosa, whose watch it was, Columbus had himself turned in half an hour before midnight. Shortly afterwards the yawning mate decided to take a nap and went to lie down, naturally telling the boy at the wheel to sing out if anything unusual should happen.

Suddenly, *Santa Maria* slid quietly up on to the reef.

Had the boy at the wheel been asleep? or had his thoughts been far away with his mother in Andalusia? Whatever it was, he only came to his senses when he noticed that the rudder was scraping against coral.

Columbus was the first up on deck. After him came the mate, and before long the decks were filled with sleepy men torn from well-earned sleep. *Santa Maria* was well and truly on the rocks and bumping with every gentle swell. They tried to warp her off, but it was no use. *Niña* had noticed the mishap and put about at once. Everything possible was done to save *Santa Maria*, but she was already past that, for every succeeding wave just carried her further up on to the reef. She slewed round so that the seas were abeam. The sharp coral perforated her stout planks, and the water began to rise in her. Columbus and the entire crew were taken aboard *Niña*.

When day dawned both crews set about salvaging her contents. The chief Guacanagari brought all his men down to the shore to help ; and, when he saw what had happened, he wept. Thanks to his help with men and so many canoes, the whole cargo and all the stores were brought ashore on Christmas day. Then *Santa Maria* was chopped up and her timbers taken ashore, bit by bit.

Niña was too small to accommodate *Santa Maria's* crew on the long homeward voyage to Spain, now soon to start ; so it was decided to build a fort with the wreckage of *Santa Maria*, provision and fit it out with her stores and weapons, and leave fifty men behind in it, that being the number of her crew. As well as the fort, they had Guacanagari's promise of friendship and protection.

In the midst of the Spaniard's grief and despair at the loss of *Santa Maria*, they saw some canoes come round the *Punta Santa* and heard the natives in them calling and stretching out their hands to let the Spaniards see the gold that lay in them.

The news of the white man's thirst for gold had spread along the coast, and those who had already been in contact with the Spaniards had told of the strange and wonderful things they had been given in exchange for gold, little tinkling bells, red cloths and glass beads. And so Guacanagari had brought hem gold. When he saw how his white friend rejoiced at the sight of it, he told him that he would give him lumps of it as large as a clenched fist ; and at that, Columbus forgot his worries, for here at last was the gold which all at home expected him to bring as proof that the world they had helped him to discover was really a *rich* new world.

Gold! The Spaniards' eyes gleamed greedily. They stood all about the shore bartering their possessions for it, while Guacanagari by signs and his interpreters gave them to understand that in the east there lay a country with a limitless wealth of gold.

Columbus took the stranding as a sign from God, with whose help he now felt certain he would eventually find his way to the land whence the yellow metal came.

There was no difficulty now in getting volunteers for the garrison of the fort which had been built on an eminence among the mangrove bushes down by the flat beach at the head of the bay by Cape Haiti. It would be a comfortable place in which to stay while Columbus and the others struggled with storms, and perhaps death, on their long voyage back to Spain. The *cacique* was an excellent fellow, the girls pretty with their light brown skins and no clothes to hide their shapely bodies, and, also, before Columbus could get back with more ships and equipment, they would have been able to have made one or two private expeditions to that country in the east and done a little work on their own in the rich gold beds in its rivers. Yes, there were volunteers enough.

The fort was named *Villa de Navidad*, after the holy festival of Christmas, and so the time came to sail back to Spain. Guacanagari and his people filled *Niña's* ship's boats with rich gifts, the luscious fruits of their island, rare timbers and spices, and, first and foremost, gold. Then they gathered on the shore to say goodbye, and with them stood fifty of Columbus' men. They had received the strictest orders to behave in an orderly manner : to keep their hands off other people's girls and wives, to be courteous and civil to the nice natives, and to help them where they could. They waved and waved until *Niña* disappeared behind the sacred point ; and the moment she was out of sight, someone said, " Come on, boys ! " and set his arm round the nearest Indian girl.

When *Niña* was well out in the bay, the Admiral saw *Pinta* coming up with a very hangdog Martin Alonzo Pinzon on her bridge. His going off on a venture of his own had not been a success. Later, there was a scene in the Admiral's cabin. Vincente Pinzon took his brother's part and there was a real row ; but Columbus would not let matters come to a head. He could not afford to quarrel with a selfish, disobedient crew, which acted against his orders. The day of reckoning must wait till he returned to Spain. And so, the two ships sailed away together with course set for Spain, leaving the wreck of *Santa Maria* behind on the coral reef.

Columbus went back to adulation and homage, to the favour of princes and the envy of the nobles, to a brief period of sunshine and an early death in poverty, humiliated and partly forgotten. Seven years after his return he was to be brought back to Spain in chains from the new world that he had discovered.

Columbus returned to Haiti and Villa de Navidad on 28th November, 1493. There were no signs of life to be seen on the shore. In some of the Indian's huts, whose owners had fled, they found a Spanish sash, a silver button, or a chiselled dagger. Then, in the immediate neighbourhood of the fort, they discovered the shrivelled bodies of eleven white men.

The Spaniards had begun by fighting among themselves—over gold and women. Several were killed in that way. Then they took to roaming about in the interior, plundering and violating as they went along. In the end, the *caciques* of the interior could stand it no longer, and so they followed the Spaniards back to the coast and overpowered the fort, giving no quarter. Although the Spaniards had assaulted the women of his own tribe, Guacanagari went so far in his loyalty to Columbus as actually to take part in the defence of the fort, by which several of his men were killed and wounded.

Columbus left the north coast of Haiti and sailed to the eastern part of the island, the present republic of San Domingo, and there at what is now its capital, Cuidad Trujillo, he set up the Spaniards' headquarters for the West Indies. There it remained until South and Central America were discovered and proved to be far richer in gold than the islands, so that the centre of gravity was shifted to the south-west.

Our *Santa Maria* was rocking at her anchor in the swell that reached her from across the fateful coral reef on which her famous namesake had come to grief. Her journey, too, was over. How graceful she looked there, like a white swan among the geese and ducks of Cape Haiti's own dirty fishing boats and little schooners.

A road has been built along the coast, but otherwise it looks very much as it must have appeared to Columbus : a flat beach running far inland, broken here and there by larger and smaller salt water lagoons, and overgrown with mangrove. There is nothing but the eminence on which Columbus built his fort, to relieve the monotony. In the background are the distant blue mountains, where you can see the grim profile of mad Henry Christophe's castle.

We were driving along the coastal road with *our* Guacanagari, the Danish Consul, who had invited us to dinner and to sample his rum which he made himself. It was our farewell to him, to Haiti, and to the islands of the West Indies.

We sat in the shade of the verandah's palm-leaf roof and watched jet-black girls coming and going with loads of waste-cane on their heads, all that remained of the rustling sugar-canes of the fields once the machetes had cut them, the women bound them, the lorries taken them to the crushing machines that pulped them, so that the greeny-yellow juice  poured down from those greedy iron jaws into the vat, from there into a pipe, and so to where it is distilled and slowly transformed into clear golden rum whose scent is reminiscent of Captain Marryat and winter evenings in the vicarage.

" Skal ", said the consul, lazily stretching out a leg and crushing a dark-brown spider the size of a child's fist. It was hairy and beastly.

" Dangerous ? " I asked.

"What, the rum?" said the consul.

"No, the spider."

"I've never been bitten by one; but it can kill a dog or a horse."

"Skal!" said we, raising our glasses to the sun.

The black girls were still passing the door in an endless stream. Then, down the road came a poor little donkey heavily laden with two large sacks of raw coffee—topped by a fat old negress smoking a pipe. It was time to be going.

We had to get back before darkness fell, because a farewell ceremony had been arranged in which we were to take part, and which I was to photograph. Guacanagari was to show us that Haiti still gave its guests a worthy farewell. Niels and Jens would already be waiting on the shore in their gala uniforms: red cap, blue sweater, and best trousers. To mark the end of the voyage, they had shaved off their beards and so no longer looked like pirates, but like the nice decent Danish fishermen that they were.

The "Caramel" was drawn up on shore, and on the road stood a little group of a dozen negroes. Only two of them were women. The tourist chief was giving them their final instructions. It was obvious, if only from the women, that he had read all about Columbus' departure. There were prettier girls in the island. None of us volunteered to stay behind; and, if we had forced Jens or Niels to remain, neither would have come to blows with the *caciques* of the interior on their account.

"Let's get started!" growled the skipper.

On this eminence Columbus built his fort

"Rich gifts" at parting : journey's end

"O.K." said I to the tourist chief, who signalled to the negroes on the road.

With stiff strides the negroes set off in procession down to the shore to deliver their "rich gifts." They were thoroughly disgruntled, because they knew that the Tourist Department would be paying them and *it*, of course, knew the tariff. Reluctantly they handed over bundles of sugar-cane, grapefruit, hens in baskets, masses of flowers, and two large bulging sacks, which the skipper, Jens and Niels duly stowed away in the "Caramel." It looked magnificent and made an excellent subject for a photograph.

What was in the sacks? I wondered rather anxiously whether it could be coffee or rice? That would almost be outdoing the real Guacanagari's farewell to Columbus. Then the last photograph on the roll was taken, and I put away my Leica.

"You may as well keep the sugar-cane and the flowers," said the tourist chief, "but I would like to have the hens and the rest back."

"It's straw in the sacks," called Jens from the "Caramel."

Half an hour later, the sails slid slowly up and *Santa Maria* began to move towards the passage through the reef.

The mainsail filled; the head-sails were right as they were. The negroes had long since left the beach and were well on their way home. The consul and the tourist chief waved once or twice, then they got into the car and drove away in a cloud of dust. Niels began peeling sweet potatoes for our evening meal.

We had a long way home. Indeed, we had.